I0420995

Crushing the Alinsky Radicals

By
Robert Villegas

Crushing the Alinsky Radicals
By
Robert Villegas

Copyright 2015 Robert Villegas, Jr.
Copyright 2020 Robert Villegas, Jr.
Published in the USA by Robert Villegas, Jr.

Second Edition

All Rights Reserved. No part of this book may be reproduced in any manner without the written permission of the copyright holder. Contact:

info@documentservicesinternational.com

www.documentservicesinternational.com

ISBN-13: 978-1517172978

ISBN-10: 1517172977

Library of Congress Control Number 2015952978

Series Title: Villegas Politics Volume 1

Dedicated to

Courage to Stand for Right

The author would like to acknowledge an intellectual debt to Ayn Rand and her philosophy Objectivism. The author is a student of her philosophy but solely responsible for his understanding of that philosophy. He is not a spokesperson for her ideas but only for his own views and opinions.

Table of Contents

Introduction

There is a specter haunting our political institutions today. This specter, for want of a better term, I call the Alinsky Radicals, a group of politicians and educators intent on taking over our freedoms and liberties. These people are in charge of our culture today because their philosophy dominates our political and educational institutions. This philosophy, essentially, puts forward both altruism and collectivism and because most people are raised on these two principles, there is very little in the way of opposition.

This particular group is associated politically, with the communists and fascists of the past. They are *not* your father's liberals. They are the direct descendants of Marxists like Che, Castro, Chavez and Maduro to mention a few. In the USA, their inspiration is a labor-trained community organizer named Saul Alinsky who operated mostly in Chicago.

I'm going to say something that few people say about progressives and Alinsky Radicals: they are medievalists. Their ideas and opinions about capitalism are essentially medieval in nature. During medieval times men thought that making a profit was evil. To make a profit was stealing. They hated merchants and others who brought us products and goods. They considered such people as dealing with the material world which meant evil because they considered the material world to be decadent and sinful. In short, medievalists think unscientifically, they foster what are called old wives tales and superstitions. They don't think clearly and mostly think in terms of concretes that are understood only on the surface of things with little in the way of concepts and "hidden truths". What *we* call "hidden truths" today was for medievalists unreal and therefore mysterious and devil-like. So, when progressives criticize profit, denigrate material success, accuse capitalists of being on the side of demons and sinister forces, they are basing these views on very primitive ideas and unscientific and illogical conclusions.

Medievalists are also traditionalists. They oppose technological progress in favor of traditional methods of living and production. This perspective belies their protestations of allegiance to science and historical understanding. When automation improves production, lowers prices and efficiently improves the use of human and mechanical energy, they oppose it as "stealing jobs", putting people out of work and harming the traditional family structure. They influence activists and politicians and, for the most part, their fallacious views are taken as "the good".

But most importantly, they have inherited from Christianity and the medievalists a general attitude about the individual that sees him as basically corrupt and self-interested. They see man as a sinner who obtains his values from a collectivist perspective that they favor. Their views about what is good and evil have poisoned their attitudes about individual initiative, individual accomplishment and especially Individual Rights. Today and for many generations in the past whenever they think about man, the individual, they think of a corrupt dirty creature who must be foiled in any activity that he or she undertakes especially if it means starting a business. This anti-man attitude is so pervasive that it negatively affects the psychology of any individual who seeks to distinguish himself in any positive way. You can see this attitude in both left and right but especially in the left.

One individual who distinguished herself as beautiful and pure was treated abysmally by those around her because of her attitude about joy and pleasure. It moved her to say the following:

"Success makes so many people hate you. I wish it wasn't that way. It would be wonderful to enjoy success without seeing envy in the eyes of those around you. – Marilyn Monroe[1]

Someone as beautiful and successful as Marilyn certainly had many admirers of her beauty and talent; but there were also others who hated her and made fun of her for standing out so attractively. This attitude of hatred comes from the envy brought into our culture by ancient attitudes towards individuals who are beautiful and talented. It is expressed by the left through its anti-capitalist and anti-individual rights attitudes. The left is particularly critical of successful capitalists who happen to work smarter and harder than most other people. Indeed, the left has no problem loving people who bow to them and give all their money away. What they hate is someone who actually earned his success and money. It is this ancient attitude that exposes the utter anti-scientific and anti-man attitude of leftist collectivists and statists. Their goal is to control and destroy the bright light of success.

Because the medieval period was heavily Christian, medievalists, during their period, operated according to entrenched views about human sacrifice and collectivism. Medieval society was broken up into collectives that worked hard to maintain their hold on serfs, guilds, lords and royalty. Each group strove to protect its turf against the others. Most men, the serfs, were taught to be obedient and to understand their place in the world as dutiful and worshipful toward the lordly classes and royalty. Guilds protected workers from the encroachment of capitalism and automation in favor of "skilled labor" and against "mass production" that was considered "worldly".

---

[1] https://www.brainyquote.com/quotes/marilyn_monroe_499749

Medievalists also fostered the principle of sacrifice. They worshipped Jesus who preached sacrifice for the poor and lordship for the royals. They completely missed the benefits of capitalism when it arrived because of their focus on the poor (who were poor because of medieval views of progress) "giving" to those in need. As capitalism began to eliminate poverty, they continued to foster the poor people that were disappearing in greater and greater numbers. To this day, they declare their love of the poor and downtrodden while the poor today live better than the kings of the medieval period because of the remnants of capitalism they still enjoy.

Consider what this attitude does to the left. Because they are so convinced that man is a sinful creature, they think he will cheat, lie, steal, kill, etc., in order to get his way. This cognitive error provides for them a justification for making life difficult for the individual who seeks to live an honest life. They feel they are morally justified in taxing, controlling, stealing from (yes criminals are part of this) and killing anyone who would seek to be successful in life. If you doubt this, read in your history books how many people Hitler, Stalin and Mao killed in the name of ridding society of intellectuals and capitalists. It is the individual and individualism that these monsters of the left, including today's progressives and Alinskly Radicals, want to destroy. When they do this, they also destroy the very people who are making the improvements in our products and lives possible.

In this book, I hope to convince you of the evil of the Alinsky Radicals and to provide the intellectual ammunition you need to eradicate them from society. The Alinsky Radicals represent a group of Marxist-minded revolutionary radicals who have infiltrated government and especially our educational system; they seek to insinuate a virulent altruism and re-distribution into our society by utilizing the philosophy of pragmatism. As pragmatists, they depict themselves as "practical" community activists offering solutions that will supposedly improve society. At the same time, they utilize "street tactics" to infiltrate neighborhoods, local schools, churches, local businesses and community centers to infuse them with the "spirit of sacrifice". These tactics include voter registration, community organizing, shakedowns of businesses, street protests and violence; all aimed at re-engineering society in order to facilitate a Marxist re-distribution of income, control of neighborhoods, and a "purge" of political opposition. They are essentially engineering a medieval form of society and calling it progress.

This book is for the younger generation (sometimes called "millennials"). It will bring a perspective that millennials are not taught in schools today. It will also resurrect a great many terms that have been dropped from their vocabularies by their teachers. I will introduce terms such as individual rights, totalitarianism, reason, liberty and others; the kinds of words the government today would prefer millennials not know.

For decades, Alinsky-style politicians have used pragmatism to whitewash the government's activities while stripping people of their fundamental rights. By not teaching young people the vocabulary of liberty, and by changing the definitions of liberty-oriented terms, they intend to take advantage of our ignorance to move society toward more oppressive controls. This book tells you how and why this is happening; and it will give you the intellectual tools you need to defend yourself.

The millennial generation is one of the most intelligent and productive economic groups in history. Unlike past generations, you are technically savvy, connected to the entire world. Indeed, all of world history is at your fingertips, a mere finger's touch away. When you are confronted by an opinion or a fact that you know little about, you can fill the gaps by means of a mere click on a tiny screen which brings you an avalanche of new knowledge in seconds. Yet, much of that knowledge is brought to you by the pragmatists of the left who want to "condition" you to collectivism and altruism. With this book, I am counting on your developing the ability to check and to challenge the ideas that the left is feeding you. I want you to investigate what is happening with your rights. I want you to use your technological tools to research philosophy, politics and education in order to understand the wider context of ideas and the movements that intend to animate change in society.

This book is intended as a primer on the Alinsky Radicals. Its basic thesis is that this group of radicals should be completely rejected by American society because of the considerable harm they do. Not only are they destroying society, they are also bringing a new nihilism.

In this book, I will not provide a comprehensive history of the progressive movement. I'm not giving you full chapters on the nuances of progressivism. Instead, I'm giving you what I call a hierarchical approach that establishes the framework for my conclusion that the Alinsky Radicals should be rejected politically. In a sense, I'm saving you years of investigation by refuting bad ideas at their source. Like a house of cards, the rest, the whole of it, will fall down. If I can refute Hegel and Marx, then the rest follows.

Nor will I provide you with a full history of Classical Liberalism, a political philosophy that fostered laissez faire capitalism. Ludwig von Mises, the central thinker of Classical Liberalism, wrote his work "Human Action" in almost 900 pages and he has written voluminously along with Hayak,

Hazlitt and others. I leave this research up to you.

For starters, I'd like to point out that almost everything you have been taught in school about politics is wrong. You may have been taught that capitalism is a system of exploitation and slavery; that it is tied to fascism or the southern slave trade. You may have been taught that your leaders are benign autocrats seeking only to help people and that capitalists are evil people intent on exploiting and plundering. They may have told you that the social contract involves sacrificing your own interests for the sake of others. You may have been taught that government is supposed to create "social justice" by means of re-distributing income. None of this is true and I hope you will take a more critical look at these ideas and develop a better understanding of them. It may save your life and those you love.

Let's be sure about one thing: I will not offer you a "conservative" alternative to progressive ideas. I am not a conservative nor am I religious in any sense of the word. My view is radical, based on reality. Likewise, I do not believe that rights are a gift from God. Nor do I believe that the human mind is incapable of ascertaining reality; and I don't base my views on the so-called "fallibility" of human thinking. I am no pragmatist and I am definitely not a Kantian clinging to duty. I offer a radical interpretation of individual rights and I have no interest in imposing any religious concepts on you. I challenge both conservatism and progressivism.

When I say that I am a radical, I mean that I hold fundamental principles. Such principles relate to man's survival (ethics) and the kind of society he should build (politics). Mine is often called a "normative" approach which means it seeks to derive an "ought" from an "is". I want to bring abstract ideas down to the level of everyday life so you can see them in action and recognize their importance.

I have much in common with our Founding Fathers in the sense that they too were radicals pursuing a normative approach to building good government. They brought a different perspective to politics that involved understanding how man survives and they sought to establish a government that liberated man so he could pursue survival and happiness without the control of the state. They did not offer what is today being called "re-distributive justice" (which is nothing more than an elaborate scheme to enslave and exploit men). Instead, when they thought about what "man" needed, they thought about individuals and what they needed in order to enjoy their lives.

In my view, we need radicals for capitalism in the USA. These radicals will foster the view that man needs liberty in order to achieve happiness. These individuals will foster fundamental philosophical truths not platitudes handed down from Karl Marx, God or John Dewey. I'm not asking you to be a protestor in the streets or to infiltrate communities. That isn't necessary. What is necessary is millions of individual minds changing their perspective on important issues and bringing new principles into their lives and into the voting booth. These new radicals do not need to become talking heads on television although some of them will become educators. Instead, they will live their lives as productive citizens who want to keep their earnings, think what they choose, love who they want, work in professions they enjoy and spend their leisure relaxing with less worry about the future.

I offer a different view of success, happiness and survival that I hope will more adequately inform your thinking and start you on the road toward truth, liberty and happiness.

Robert Villegas, Jr.

Addendum to the second edition:

Much has happened in our country since the transition from President Obama to President Trump. Seeing that their policies were rejected by voters in 2016, the Alinsky Radicals have tried to absorb moderate liberals into their ranks without success. Yet, they have succeeded in hijacking the Democratic Party because the moderates were dazed by the victory of Trump and they could not come up with valid arguments to many of his ill-advised policies. They only thing that they could come up with was impeachment of Trump.

Additionally, something happened with the advent of Trumpism. People became angry at the Democrats because of their new radicalism and their unwillingness to compromise on anything. The result was that the left doubled-down and went full totalitarian. They proposed various "measures" that included virtually every program they had ever proposed before in order to flood the political debate with only leftist proposals, most of which were unworkable, costly and would give the government virtual control of the entire economy and the lives of every American. The impeachment of Donald Trump was the culmination of the swing to the looney left.

Why did people elect Donald Trump, a non-politician with years of experience in the business world? Trump was politically incorrect in the extreme and he proposed a complete dismantlement of all the money laundering schemes the Democrats had put in place. He was distasteful and had a visceral disdain for progressive ideas because he saw through them. Since he had experience with several high-level Democrats (Bill and Hillary Clinton among them), he knew of the corruption they had been involved in and he promised to "drain the swamp" of corruption that had grown up over the years.

There are essentially two segments of progressivism. First there are the "idealists" who believe all of the claptrap of altruism, the idea that they are lovers of the poor, helpers of those who can't help themselves and collectivists who want to create a utopian society based upon self-sacrifice. Certainly, they are wrong about their ideals because they are impractical. Secondly, there are the pragmatists among the progressives who practice "realpolitik". This group assumes the mantle of altruism, like the idealists but they also practice hardball politics and insist that government engage in coercion regardless of consequences. This group practices violent revolution, agitation, the Big Lie and constant denigration of their political enemies.

What many average citizens disagreed with, in electing Trump, is the relentless and unnecessary agitation done by these groups, usually funded by leftist billionaires, to accomplish leftist goals regardless of whether the bulk of the American citizenry supports it. It is essentially a cultural and political coup.

This second factor is where people such as Saul Alinsky come in. Alinsky, as a union organizer transitioned to community organizing using the methods of "realpolitik" to "overthrow" the capitalist system through various coercive means as expressed in his rules for radicals. These are not the rules of an idealist preaching a "social democracy" but of an agitator seeking to destroy and disrupt the freest elements of our society.

Yet, the true grandfather of the ideas of Alinsky is Thomas

Dewey, the philosopher who proposed pragmatism and this is where we gain an understanding about the philosophies behind progressivism. Essentially, we have Marx, Lenin and Dewey.

What we see on the modern scene are liberals who only preach the "goodness" of sacrifice and declare themselves to be advocating for benign programs that "help people". These people, unknowingly, provide the cover for the radicals who latch onto the same beliefs while also looking for power, wealth and fame – by any means necessary.

And this is where I and others who advocate reason come in. Our goal is truth not politics, freedom not statism. We seek to understand, first, reality and secondly, how man survives, and by extension, how man should interact and associate with other men. This view does not hold that capitalism is exploitative and part of a global conspiracy. Capitalism is essentially the view that man, a creature of reason, survives by means of knowing reality and dealing with other men through cooperation and trade.

If you'd like to understand better how philosophy influences life and how specific philosophers created the foundations for our modern movements, I'd suggest you read my books:

What Harvard and Princeton Don't Want you to Know (https://amzn.to/2XvkLZY) and

What's Wrong with the Corporation? (https://amzn.to/2UZrTfg)

A Concise History of How We Got Here

The closest our country came to full laissez faire capitalism was during the 19th Century when capitalist titans such as Rockefeller (1839-1937), Edison (1847-1931), Vanderbilt (1794-1877), Bell (1847-1922) and Carnegie (1835-1919) created the foundation for much of our present industrial infrastructure. This was a time when Horatio Alger (1832-1899) wrote his "rags-to-riches" stories that inspired young men to industry, hard work and honesty. Everywhere during this period new towns were sprouting as the manufacturing, steel, oil, mining and forestry industries attracted workers from around the globe.

It was a time fueled by new energy sources, new machines and new ideas that revolutionized living standards and created a dynamic optimism that portended greater times ahead. This period laid the foundation for much that we take for granted today. In fact, one can say that if it were not for the "unfettered" capitalist 19th century, we would not have most of the conveniences we enjoy today. Indeed, even the poorest among us live better than the pampered kings of yesteryear; and some say that the last decade (2010-2020) produced the best living standard in world history to date. [2]

However, we do not have a capitalist system today. Ours is a mixed economy with a combination of freedom and regulation. So, the question to ask is: "If 19th Century capitalism was so good for us, why did we turn away from it even while we were enjoying its benefits?"

---

[2]https://www.spectator.co.uk/2019/12/weve-just-had-the-best-decade-in-human-history-seriously/

One reason was that Modern philosophy had declared man the property of the state. This development virtually ignored the earth-shattering innovation that individual rights had brought to the world. Intellectuals dismissed man's rights in favor of the Kantian revolution that preached duty and categorical imperatives. This brought about a 20th Century rife with totalitarianism, world wars, mass murder and economic collapse.

It was during the 20th Century that communism killed millions in its quest to create a new man who would habitually sacrifice for the collective. Fascism in Nazi Germany killed millions of Jews and other nationalities in order to create the pure racial collective. Mao massacred millions in his purges in order to rid China of "profiteers" so he could expropriate their luxurious homes.

On the other hand, the Enlightenment view of man held that he was an autonomous individual who possessed rights that could not be infringed and that the purpose of government was to protect those rights rather than violate them. On an isolated island an ocean away from Europe, limited government was invented to protect liberty; not direct man's actions.

Economically, liberty was expressed as capitalism, a system that enabled men to trade freely and keep the results of their labor. Capitalism provided jobs, new products, enjoyment and abundance for those who chose to participate in the American dream. The *real* suffrage movement was about individual rights and it was waged by the Founding Fathers. Their time, however, was short. Modern philosophy brought a hatchet to the discussion.

The impetus toward capitalism was destroyed when Kant[3] and others started gaining influence in America. It started in the mid-19th century, when followers of Hegel, Karl Marx and Friedrich Engels began portraying capitalism as exploitation, theft and tyranny. They even claimed that capitalism was the cause of poverty. These views were bolstered by Marx who claimed that socialism was inevitable and that hastening its ascendency through violent revolution was proper. Others countenanced an "incremental" approach in the march toward socialism.

Marxists and other leftists argued that economic regulation (coercion) was necessary to restrain free market competition. By this view, "unbridled competition" and selfishness were seen as dangerous to society and only government, a dictatorship of the proletariat, could ensure "the public good".

Mises[4] tells us:

"…the basic conception of Socialism had been quite clearly worked out in the course of the second quarter of the nineteenth century by those writers designated by Marxism as "Utopian Socialists." Schemes for a socialist order of society were extensively discussed at that time, but the discussion did not go in their favour. The Utopians had not succeeded in planning social structures that would withstand the criticism of economists and sociologists. It was easy to pick holes in their schemes; to prove that a society constructed on such principles must lack efficiency and vitality, and that it certainly would not come up to expectations…

"It was at this moment that Marx appeared. Adept as he was in Hegelian dialectic — a system easy of abuse by those who

---

[3] The Critique of Pure Reason and The Metaphysic of Morals
[4] Ludwig von Mises, Austrian economist

seek to dominate thought by arbitrary flights of fancy and metaphysical verbosity — he was not slow in finding a way out of the dilemma in which socialists found themselves. Since Science and Logic had argued against Socialism, it was imperative to devise a system which could be relied on to defend it against such unpalatable criticism. This was the task which Marxism undertook to perform. It had three lines of procedure. First, it denied that Logic is universally valid for all mankind and for all ages. Thought, it stated, was determined by the class interests. The type of reasoning which had refuted the socialist idea was "revealed" as "bourgeois" reasoning, an apology for Capitalism. Secondly, it laid it down that the dialectical development led of necessity to Socialism, that the aim and end of all history was the socialization of the means of production by the expropriation of the expropriators — the negation of negation. Finally, it was ruled that no one should be allowed to put forward, as the Utopians had done, any definite proposals for the construction of the Socialist Promised Land. Since the coming of Socialism was inevitable, Science would best renounce all attempt to determine its nature"[5]

Finally, Marxist revolutionaries doubled-down on morality and added altruism, "from each according to his ability, to each according to his needs". This justified using force to make men sacrifice for the sake of the collective. This is what destroyed capitalism.

The Enlightenment argument for individual rights and capitalism meant nothing during a time when altruism provided the moral blinders that kept people ignorant about what was really happening to their economic lives. Men were being robbed because history had decreed robbery to be a matter of historical necessity. Reality? Facts? What were they

---

[5] Socialism by Ludwig von Mises, Liberty Classics Hardcover, Page 6

against a long line of generational altruists who preached force as the solution to all man's problems? I've seen the testimony for this system: the rubble outside of Munich and the concentration camp at Dachau.

Fast Forward to the 1960s and '70s. The members of the violent communist group known as the Weather Underground, realizing that their bombings and murders would not defeat capitalism, adopted a virulent form of incrementalism. Their adherence to the Cloward-Piven[6] strategy, which fostered "stressing the system" (by registering thousands for the welfare rolls) moved them into community organizing. In New York, the welfare rolls swelled to such a point that government coffers were indeed stressed. This was incrementalism in leaps and bounds.

Additionally, by going into the universities and concentrating on education, they were able to create new generations of like-minded radicals who could spread Cloward-Piven strategies under the auspices of the Alinsky Radicals.

Saul Alinsky was a legendary communist organizer who learned his methods from gangsters and union organizers in Chicago. His strategy, the subject of his book "Rules for Radicals", involved organizing collectives within poor neighborhoods and agitating for reforms that re-distributed money and government services to the collectives.

Essentially, the Alinsky Radicals had perfected the revolutionary tactic of "shakedown" where government agencies and corporations were threatened with bad publicity, protests, boycotts and destruction if they did not cater to the "needs" of the community agitators. Essentially, these tactics were designed to lead to various forms of re-distribution of

---

[6] https://en.wikipedia.org/wiki/Cloward%E2%80%93Piven_strategy

money and services. Long-term, they led to "white flight" from the neighborhoods as businesses sought to escape the unfair shakedowns.

Not only was the shakedown strategy short-term but it led to even worse conditions in the neighborhoods due to business flight which destroyed jobs. Like any oppressive system that is doomed to fail, the only way to keep the community bonanza going was to expand to other neighborhoods nationwide.

ACORN, an organization closely tied to a community organizer named Barak Obama, expanded into those other neighborhoods to train people to become professional parasites. The strategy also called for them to get into politics so they could re-distribute even larger sums from the taxpayers to their radical friends and leftist fellow-travelers.

So, the radicals who were experts at operating outside the system (to bring it down) now became part of the system (to bring it down). The contradiction for them was that once inside the system, voters (who were not communists) expected that the government should still run smoothly. They (the radicals) had to appear to be making things better.

Once in charge of the system, they were beholden to a new constituency; the dissatisfied voter who could vote them out. This was a hard position for a revolutionary who didn't care about productive citizens as evidenced by President Obama's grudging efforts to actually make government work. I'm sure he asked himself, "How can I bring the system down when I need to win the next election?" (Obvious solution: rule by Executive Decree and blame the "emergency" you have created on the other guys).

Yet, the most disheartening aspect of this pragmatic strategy was obvious once they gained full power with Obama. Their socialist "principles" of re-distribution did not result in the vibrant economy they promised. No magic abundance was created. The world that came after "change" was a slum. The more power they gained, the worse things became for the poor.

The inability of the Alinsky Radicals to rule an economy is not just a human failing. There is an aspect of Marxism that creates this condition. Marxists fail because Marxism is unworkable. The idea of one group making all the key decisions for millions of individuals can only fail. Men are not made to be dutiful, obedient drones.

For example, Obama was good at getting elected but ineffectual at actually running government as is evidenced by his numerous scandals and criminal acts. Whenever he sought to address a problem, his immediate solution was sacrifice for the rest of us but not for his friends. Private investors were told to give up their 401Ks for the sake of Chrysler, taxpayers were forced to pay higher taxes for a failed stimulus program and re-distribution continued to replace investment with ever higher deficit spending. Waste, fraud, extensions of unemployment benefits, expansion of the Food Stamp program, all of these are interventions that not only violated individual rights, but also violated the law of supply and demand. It is no wonder that economic growth virtually ground to a halt under Obama.

Obama's failures were not new. Wherever communism or socialism have been tried, these systems failed utterly and the only thing the leaders could do was blame the failures of their new order on the old order, much like President Obama blames George Bush for the failures of his own administration and much like the Soviets blamed the bourgeoisie for the failures of communism.

This is par for the course among radical leftists. Rather than question the correctness and viability of their own ideas, they want to find someone to blame for their failures. Rather than admit they are wrong, the argument must be that if you aren't with us you are against us.

One would think that a rational politician would see the long-term value of "doing the right thing" such as lowering taxes (or eliminating them), reducing the deficit and the size of government and eliminating onerous regulations (all of them). But these changes, even if a radical President like Obama would do them, would take too long to bear fruit. The better economy would come too late to influence the next election. Rather than get elected by doing the right thing for the economy (austerity), this President would rather buy votes using huge tax expenditures that will make the long-term situation worse. As Keynes said, "In the long-run, we are all dead."

Today's Alinsky Radicals are grappling with the same issue as the Leninists once did in Soviet Russia; but with a twist. Leninists thought that a perfect society would result from their killing all capitalist remnants (people). We know now that this did not happen and millions of people were needlessly sacrificed for a Utopian dream that never materialized.

The Alinsky Radicals, following their fascist predecessors, thought that the solution for economic malaise was to work with favored businesses that paid them off. To affect this, they became Keynesian technocrats, graph analysts and button pushers who thought they were smart enough to make things work.

Keynesian theories helped them lie to themselves that force was an effective economic tool. They thought they could stimulate economic activity by printing more money, bring about lower prices by quantitative easing, pick winners and losers and increase average individual income by increasing the minimum wage, etc., etc. For every economic "need" they offered a fallacious form of coercion to make things better. All magic is sleight of hand.

The truth is that no group of technocrats is smart enough to regulate the thousands upon thousands of transactions engaged by people every day. Had the leftists wanted to learn why their policies didn't work, they could have read Mises who would have told them that freedom, not coercion, will create economic growth.

Calling our present system "fascism" is not a spurious criticism. Fascism is a well-defined *economic* system characterized by a so-called government/business compromise that breeds corruption, ever higher taxes, crony-socialism (sometimes falsely called crony-capitalism), regulations, shakedowns, autocracy and a disregard for individual rights.

Fascism, to be precise, is not a kind of capitalism but a kind of socialism which brings with it all the negatives associated with government control of production, monetary manipulation, price inflation, misallocation of resources and the violation of the law of supply and demand. In a fascist system property rights are retained by citizens but the government instructs businesspeople on how to run their businesses.

This is all done, supposedly, for the sake of the "public good" but for some reason, the public never sees the good. If you study the history of fascism, you'll learn that in the early part of the 20th century, fascism was considered a superior system. Leftists all over the spectrum, including some highly prominent business tycoons, admired Mussolini's fascist system and even thought Hitler was doing wonders for the German economy. American intellectuals openly praised fascism and politicians tried to institute fascist principles into the American economy.

Even today, without using the word fascism, many politicians praise the idea of government/business cooperation. Hillary Clinton and others openly praised it and promised to make it "work". It takes a village, she said. What she really meant is it takes a village with a large corporation under the thumb of the government; her thumb.

The result of the Obama economy was decimation. Billions of dollars were borrowed, spent and re-distributed to people who did not want to work. The budget deficits grew massively while investment capital was being hoarded by corporations in the form of cash until the government took on a saner policy. Companies refused to invest in jobs because of government employment policies such as EEOC, National Labor Relations Board, the EPA, Obamacare and Dodd-Frank financial regulations. The goal of businesses became, not to expand and prosper, but to save money and stay alive.

The rise of Alinsky radicals in government created a considerable backlash among "conservative" Americans who have split from mainstream conservatism and neo-conservatism. These new (nearly capitalist) radicals said "enough" to progressive encroachments and tried to return to the Enlightenment concept of "individual rights". Bolstered by Ayn Rand's political philosophy and free market arguments, Tea Party Americans fought back and tried to end the oppression of progressivism.

However, the dilemma for the Tea Party was that most of them were religious conservatives. Conservatism, in particular, evangelical conservatism, merely seeks to impose another form of tyranny, a theocracy that follows the Ten Commandments and a distorted view of liberty based almost exclusively on religious morality. Under the guise of fighting for religious freedom, they fight against atheism and abortion; and they liken secular Americans to communists who want to destroy "American values". They ridicule even those secularists who foster individual rights and capitalism.

If economic secularists of today are not able to throw off the religious conservatism of many of its members, this will prove harmful to our country. To avoid this collapse, New Capitalist Radicals (who espouse individual rights) must stand up and stop the slide into socialism, reduce the debt and reinstitute the Constitution.

Our country is now being led by Alinsky Radicals even though they lost the last election. This is because of their hold on the "deep state" government and their dominance of our educational system. Either they will hold on to power by nefarious means or they will struggle to disrupt and destroy the society that rejects them. They will not go quietly into the night.

This is why they must be crushed politically.

Who was Alinsky?

"The villainy you teach me, I will execute, and it shall go hard but I will better the instruction." – William Shakespeare, The Merchant of Venice

Who was Saul Alinksy?

He was a "community organizer" who started his work in the old stockyards neighborhood in Chicago. For Alinsky, it was unquestionable that America needed change and he had no qualms about the morality of his quest to bring that change about. In his mind, capitalism was an evil system and the poor were the means by which he could force the capitalists to serve society rather than profits.

But as "noble" as his ends might have been, this is not what Alinsky was about. He was a pragmatist from Chicago, a practitioner of "realpolitik" where political action was about power and getting it by any means necessary. His teachers were the mob bosses and union bosses of Chicago who fixed elections and bought votes by controlling the neighborhoods and running them as their own personal fiefdoms.

About Alinsky, we read, "The Back-of-the-Yards neighborhood, setting of Upton Sinclair's The Jungle, was an immense slum in the shadows of Chicago's giant Union Stockyards, one of the largest factory complexes ever created. Its inhabitants were poor; they had no rights and no job security. In the course of one year, wages were cut three times. As Alinsky watched and decided that he could no longer stand by as a silent observer.

"He believed that widespread poverty left America open to the influence of demagogues and that the only antidote was active, widespread participation in the political process. Alinsky envisioned an "organization of organizations," comprised of all sectors of the community - youth committees, small businesses, labor unions and, most influential of all, the Catholic Church."[7]

For Alinsky, the doctrine of capitalist evil was a device used to justify any act against capitalist property ownership. So, it is with a questioning mind that I reproduce the statement that "In the course of one year, wages were cut three times" in "The-Back-of-the-Yards" neighborhood. The likelihood is that there was no actual exploitation going on in this neighborhood. The actions of the corporations were the result of market forces, not a desire to exploit or impoverish people. Indeed, for anti-capitalists, success comes from inventing "the evils of capitalism". They could only use falsehoods to justify their interventions, their shakedowns and their regulations.

Saul Alinsky was a dishonest actor who used the idea of capitalist exploitation to manipulate poor people. His efforts to "help the poor" were nothing more than a tactic designed to "milk the system" and muscle in on corporate profits. His "cause" of anti-capitalism was about re-distributing the profits of capitalist production. The result was that both the poor and capitalist property owners were reduced to seeking survival with a blood-sucking worm slowly eating their substance. That worm is called, for Alinsky, community organizing.

From a macro-economic perspective, the neighborhood had been impacted by the great depression. Competent economic analysis places the blame for the depression on the Federal government, not on local Chicago capitalist entities.[8] There is nothing the neighborhood, including the capitalists, could

---

[7] http://archive.itvs.org/democraticpromise/alinsky.html
[8] For a good explanation of it read the book "The Forgotten Man" by Amity Shlaes.

have done to avert the disasters wrought by the depression.

During the Great Depression, capitalism was not responsible for the condition of the people. The government was responsible, specifically banking policies and later Hoover's tariffs (the Smoot-Hawley Bill).[9] People were losing jobs all over the country and purchasing ground to a halt. To think that a nationwide joining of community groups could impact that massive social upheaval in any positive way is poor economic thinking. What could the workers in The-Back-of-the-Yards do? How could boycotts improve their condition when corporate entities were struggling to stay afloat by reducing expenses? How could strikes, demonstrations and even negotiations change the overall economic condition that was rampant throughout the country?

Yet, for Saul Alinsky, the culprit was profit and profit-seeking. In his mind, this concept was evil. He thought that men who pursued profit did so solely at the expense of the workers. For Alinsky, the depression was caused by evil corporate acts and his only answer was to curtail the profits of the capitalists – which was no solution at all. Corporations, in his mind, had unlimited funds that had been stolen from the workers; funds that belonged to the workers. Needless to say, this view has several sources including the Catholic doctrine against usury and merchants, Karl Marx's anti-capitalism, Immanuel Kant's duty, Auguste Comte's altruism and John Dewey's pragmatism. Ultimately, the source of Alinsky's ideas was the primitive concept known as human sacrifice, the requirement that the individual should sacrifice himself to the needs and values of the collective.

We will explore the wrong-headedness of Marxism in another

---

[9] https://www.thoughtco.com/causes-of-the-great-depression-104686

chapter but it is clear that Alinsky was a Marxist who held that the community had a moral right to fight and thwart the self-interest of any capitalist entity.

The short-sighted activist approach of Alinsky could never work. Companies need profits in order to stay alive. They need profits in order to invest in their businesses and create new jobs. Society should properly function with a minimum of conflict and harm. Agitation, protest and conflict only make things worse in a system designed for cooperation and mutual advantage. No socialist agitator can make society better except to the extent that he or she desists from protesting innocent capitalists.

Corporate for-profit entities are dependent upon free markets. They need people to freely choose to do business with them and this requires marketing, advertising, product demonstrations and customers who actually enjoy or benefit from their products…all making their own decisions. Every transaction, whether it is an individual sale, labor agreement or corporate alliance, is private, voluntary and contractual. If one party is unhappy with how a transaction is being addressed, he has the right to go elsewhere or seek a change in the agreement. The contract is the central element of all social relationships and economic trades. It should never be meddled with by government or community organizers.

Any intervention into contractual relationships is essentially an effort to invalidate contracts. It is an effort to change the rules and eliminate the voluntary nature of business transactions. It says, in effect, that one party is no longer allowed to pursue its self-interest and must sacrifice its interest to the goals of the other party. It also says that the business entity must unwillingly remain in the contract.

Alinsky Radicals routinely seek the violation of contract. First, they "collectivize" the community by turning it into a political entity. Next, they ask all community members to join in a "unified" effort to negotiate all private agreements with the company. Any individual who seeks to have his own "private" agreement with the company is denied any benefits.

The community organizer creates a "social" organization that presumably "represents" the community. He creates a collective or a political entity that works to foster the goals of the community at the expense of profit-seeking entities. The larger the politicized community, the more power it can accumulate and the more damage it does to the community.

The real problem, however, is when the community organizer has an agenda not related to the good of the group. For instance, with the Alinsky organizers, it is clear that their agenda is Marxism. Their goal is to participate in the "worker's revolution" fostered by Marx and Engels. This means all interactions in the community are part of the class struggle to defeat capitalism. The goal is to turn the members of the community into a group of agitators who will challenge "the man" and insist that he make payouts to them. If a particular company does not pay tribute to the community organization, then it could be boycotted, protested and brought to the attention of politicians who could harass the company and seek to harm its reputation. This is where the rubber meets the road, so to speak, and where the paycheck comes in for the community organizer.

Once the collective is organized, it can identify targets and begin agitating for change. The more people in membership, the more power it can develop. By analyzing the focus of power within companies and organizations, they can identify which entities are ripe for exploitation. This would include banks, financial institutions, franchised restaurants, large retail establishments and large corporate employers such as factories and service organizations whose profits run into the millions of dollars.

Alinsky perfected his organizing tactics on the streets of Chicago and wrote a book called "Rules for Radicals" to help educate other organizers on the "How to" of organizing communities. This book served as a handbook for community organizers for decades. Our recent President, Barack Obama once taught these tactics in Chicago and has succeeded in being the first community organizer President of the United States. By carefully orchestrating local outrage against stores and banks, he used shakedown tactics to cut into their profits. In some cases, the end result was overall impoverishment of the communities and corporate flight.

The bottom line of community organizing is muscling in on the profits of companies. These efforts will always backfire. The violation of the principle of contract destroys companies and neighborhoods. Re-distribution is immoral and no moral business will put up with it over the long-run. In some cases, they can't put up with it and must close. In other cases, they go where the climate is better, where they are not viewed as evil exploiters but as providers of value. The communities they leave are devastated.

Blighted neighborhoods like those in Chicago and Detroit are the work of Karl Marx and Saul Alinsky. After having destroyed many cities, community organizations can only expand their activities into more prosperous locations. They survive only through special preferences, more violent riots and lawsuits. They take their shakedown tactics to the national level and look for other communities to destroy such as Ferguson, Missouri and Baltimore, Maryland to name a few. With the help of people like George Soros, they move to other countries and milk them as well.

The Disvalue of the Left and the Right

Before we deal with the professional parasites of the left, I want to say at this point that there are some well-intentioned "liberals" who think that progressivism is about helping people. I know some of you and you always seem to be the first to object to my assigning evil to the Alinsky Radicals. As nice as these liberals are, they seem to ignore the fact that re-distribution, in and of itself, is theft and a violation of the individual rights of the able and productive (rich). They think that expropriating money from people who would just as soon keep the money they earn is something we do voluntarily and, because of this, it is ok – nothing more than the social contract. Everyone loves the social contract, right? NO.

To these liberals, I say, I'm certain you are exactly as you say; trying to do some good. You may not have questioned the altruism you grew up with or you may not see the harm of "a little" forced charity. Your parents may have been good-hearted people who often gave to charity and volunteered to help less affluent people. You have come to think that your parents' particular version of altruism is something benign, something you voluntarily want to do. But, I dare to say, it is time to question your pre-conceived notions.

I must point out that there is one principle all "liberals" advocate. Liberals believe that people do not have the right to keep their own earnings. Regardless of whether you advocate a little theft or a lot, it is still theft and on that basis it is immoral. This is a fact no liberal or progressive can deny: They do not believe that individuals have property rights.

In this sense, it doesn't matter whether they are good hearted people because being good-hearted toward the poor is not the same as being good-hearted toward the productive. Being nice, volunteering and all those "good" actions on behalf of others, pale in comparison to the fact that progressives (even nice progressives) advocate expropriation of money from honest people.

Yet, this idea of taking only a "little" from the rich may have applied at one time (when we were taking only a little) but it does not apply today. Today, that "little" is huge and it grows every day, to the point that there can't possibly be enough people to spend all that money on. It should also be obvious by now that the "little" being taken, the regulations being imposed and the massive government programs that grow bigger day-by-day should have long ago wiped out all poverty – but they have not. Instead, there are now more needy people than ever. When will the sacrificing stop? When will altruism have done its job of eradicating poverty? When will you start questioning just what the government is doing if it is not helping those who still, according to our leaders, need help? Where did all the money go?

Over $13 Trillion dollars have been spent on the War on Poverty and there are still nearly as many poor today as there was during the '60s.

It is time for you to wake up and consider what I and some others are saying; socialism, even a little socialism, is not only a failed system, but it operates according to the flawed idea of human sacrifice. If you respect the Constitution, even just a little, you must by now realize that the promise of a little bit of re-distribution has not been met and it is time for well-meaning liberals to realize that they are being dragged, not even kicking and screaming, into a vast dictatorship. I'm sure that is not what you had in mind with your good intentions.

It is time to say that socialism has failed. It has not failed marginally but totally. Our leaders must stop lusting after riches produced by the competent people among us. We must begin to value individual rights and individual achievement. The looting must stop. As the famous (movie) Greek said to the Persian conqueror, I say to the left: "If you understood what was honourable in life, you would avoid lusting after what belongs to others."[10]

Lusting after what belongs to others is the essence of today's leftist radicals: they hold a totally cavalier disregard for the rights and persons of individuals. They are not intellectual leaders because they do not set intellectual trends; rather they follow major philosophical trends and leverage them to gain power. One of the major trends they exploit is altruism which gives them a faux moral authority to dictate our goals.

Using altruism as a moral guide, leftists argue that sacrifice for the collective enables society to attain a sort of utopia known as the "social contract society" or "social welfare society" that is considered good because, after all, it is based upon a "voluntary" contract. Yet, this principle gives rise to the second trend which the left uses to justify its oppressions. This is pragmatism of which one principle is "the end justifies the means." The "end" here is the utopian society that altruism is supposed to create. Since this idea is "good", then doing anything, including lying, killing, manipulating and coercing are all fine as long as it is the left which is using them. But what if altruism and pragmatism do not bring about utopia?

The promise of such a society is that all human needs will be met by the government if, and only if, each individual does his best to contribute his energy and labor to the collective pot which has no bottom.

---

[10] King Leonidas

There is almost no one in society today who disagrees with the leftist call to sacrifice and this very fact gives the Alinsky Radicals their power. They have stepped into the moral vacuum left by conservatives who weakly dissent from social contract theory. The only argument provided against the radicals is that any such sacrifice must be voluntary or have free market elements. This is the equivalent of giving to the radicals the reins of the socialist wagon that is now running at top speed out of control.

On the other hand, conservatives see reality and knowledge as divinely acquired. They offer the ideas that man learns through revelation from God, that proper ethics is self-sacrificial, that science is an enemy while history is dictated by God's plan. Conceding that point of self-sacrifice to the left, they offer few arguments against the progressives' pragmatic politics because, at base, they hold the same views but in a religious form. Regarding individual rights, their view that rights are a gift from God destroys their ability to make a reasoned case for man's rights. They think that the mere suggestion that rights are derived from God is as solid an argument as can be made and this makes it impossible for them to defend rights on a rational base.

Conservatives don't realize that their idea that God is the source of rights loses more voters than it gains. Further, this idea leads them to advocate for and propose a theocracy where Christianity is considered the foundation of all rights. They ignore the fact that one could just as easily justify dictatorship using these same arguments. They wonder why they are unable to gain support among the college educated and the media. It is not the media's fault that journalists and intellectual leaders ignore conservative arguments; it is the conservatives' fault because they are unable to offer an argument that does not include mysticism.

The only arguments left for conservatives are the Classical Liberal arguments proposed by such luminaries as Hazlitt, Mises and Hayak. But these views are not without problems either; which is why they were rejected long ago. Classical Liberals preach what they think is an unassailable argument that socialism violates economic laws and, because so, it has been totally refuted. True, socialism doesn't work but merely saying so is not enough. Without a moral argument for capitalism, defensible in terms of reality, there is no argument for capitalism that can defeat socialism.

Ayn Rand disagreed with both the Classical economists and conservatives on that very point. She held that economics cannot be separated from values. She might likely ask, "What is it that you pursue when you buy something? A value." Values are central to living and economic calculations. Rand clearly saw the effort to divorce economics from values as a failed effort and the very reason that the conservatives and Classical economists were failing in the fight for capitalism – and she told them so.

Knowledge, facts, statistics cannot be politically motivating unless you answer the question, "'Knowledge' to support what value? 'Facts' to support what action? 'Statistics' to bolster which position?" Capitalism is about the pursuit of values and morality tells you how to define those values. How can mere statistics beat that? It can't.

Although, most conservatives don't realize this, their view of economics leads to the same point as the pragmatists who are so influential among politicians and businesspeople today. It is the pragmatists who developed the idea that we could determine correct action by means of cold valueless calculations and eventually, they thought, this leads to the common good, which is the collectivist idea to which both liberals and conservatives went.

The idea that you could only determine correct economic action through results devoid of values inevitably leads to the common good. It is central to the Classical Liberal's basic premises. The idea that you can prove that capitalism works best through statistics is what conservatives and Classical economists stand on. Rand simply says, true, but it is not enough. If you have no value (or moral argument) to support your economics arguments, adherence to "results" that "work", is nothing more than an empty compromise.

How do pragmatists evaluate what works? That is a problem the pragmatists answered by saying "the common good" and "collective benefit". Even they, like Mises, could not divorce their views from values, so they all went along with the prevailing value theory of the day: altruism. For them, of course, capitalism is more efficient than socialism; but capitalism is evil and that is a moral judgment. In other words, to both progressives and conservatives, capitalism is valueless.

Mises' Praxeology inevitably must become pragmatism. Here is his definition:

"Praxeology is a theoretical and systematic, not a historical, science. Its scope is human action as such, irrespective of all environmental, accidental, and individual circumstances of the concrete acts. Its cognition is purely formal and general without reference to the material content and the particular features of the actual case. It aims at knowledge valid for all instances in which the conditions exactly correspond to those implied in its assumptions and inferences. Its statements and propositions are not derived from experience. They are, like those of logic and mathematics, a priori. They are not subject to verification or falsification on the ground of experience and facts." [11]

That divorcing of economics from experience is the starting point of pragmatism. By this standard, values are arbitrary and unscientific. Also, remember that altruism and the common good is where the conservatives and the neocons end up today. They are still not convincing anyone, just as Rand said. The standard of the Kantians who believed that all value judgments were arbitrary and unscientific is the same standard as the God Father of free markets (Mises).

The only way conservatives are going to start winning votes is by talking about the morality of liberty, the fact that liberty leaves men free and this freedom is the source of a proper morality. As things stand, religion is why conservatives will never (or seldom) argue for individual liberty. Individual liberty means disobeying God and the only freedom that religion countenances is the freedom to believe in God and follow his commandments. So, whenever the conservatives bring their religious premises into the political fray, they look ignorant and philosophically backward.

For capitalism and individual rights to win the day, a new morality of individualism must come to the fore and its advocates must be adept at refuting the fallacies of socialism and central planning. They must consistently oppose altruism and stand on principle without giving away liberty through piecemeal compromises over freedom.

The progressives are riding the wave of intellectual developments put in place by Kant, Hegel, Marx and others. These radicals use a combination of a promised utopia to

---

[11] Ludwig von Mises, Human Action: A Treatise on Economics

institute a program of self-sacrifice and elimination of political enemies. The leftists today match the Leninists of the Soviet Union with their policy that the end justifies the means. Like the Leninists in Russia, they have no intention of losing in their struggle for control of America. In fact, "Lenin once famously declared that 'an organization of real revolutionaries will stop at nothing to rid itself of an unworthy member.'"[12]

The truth is that the world would have been better off without the interventions, cruelties and mass murders of the socialists of the last century. Had intellectuals and politicians not pursued the diminishment of capitalism, the world would have proceeded to make remarkable progress and people would have become more affluent, enjoyed better and more efficient products, seen more amazing entertainments and used faster, safer transportation. Even the poor would no longer be considered poor by our standards today. People would be experiencing more freedoms, more knowledge and significantly better lives.

Why do I say this? Capitalism is not a system of exploitation and increasing poverty. On the contrary, capitalism is the opposite of exploitation, slavery and child labor. Capitalism releases all individuals to live their lives for their own sakes and gives them the broadest possible range of choices including the choice to accumulate capital savings.

Capitalism holds that people belong to themselves. The result is that trade, production, capital accumulation and other forms of savings are protected by rational contract law and mutually beneficial trade.

---

[12] E. A. Rees, *Political Thought from Machiavelli to Stalin Revolutionary Machiavellism* (New York: Palgrave MacMillan, 2004), P 99 – Footnote provided by Vladimir Tismaneanu in *The Devil in History, Communism, Fascism, and some lessons of the Twentieth Century*, University of California Press, 2012

The charges against capitalism made by leftists are partly lies and partly misinterpretation of history. Many early capitalists were not reared on the philosophy of capitalism and they made some irrational decisions within a system that protected individual rights. Additionally, some of the charges made against capitalism were made during the transition period between the earlier feudal system and the developing Laissez Faire system. Capitalism was in the process of overthrowing these earlier coercive systems when it was blamed by the Marxists for wrongs such as child labor and poor factory conditions. In fact, capitalism was beginning to improve these holdovers of the feudal system when it was wrongly blamed for them. Some capitalists also did not understand the nature of capitalism and chose to engage in poor treatment of workers. Only capitalism, because it leaves people free, has the feature that enables men to correct their own mistakes and, because it creates profits, it provides companies with the resources to create ever better working conditions as well as wipe out the "need" for child labor.

If we are going to save America and restore freedom, we must counter the leftists by removing them from power - totally. One way to do this, in part, is to offer a vision of the future that not only promises a better life for the individual but delivers that better life.

Capitalism is the only system that can bring a better life because it is the only system that removes coercion from economic affairs. Rather than offer coercive re-distribution of other peoples' money, a capitalist system leaves men free to create their own affluence by means of reason[13], education, hard work, honesty and productive ability. This vision must be practical, defensible and provable. It involves a philosophic revolution that is founded in reality.

---

[13] The use of man's mind to understand reality.

Below are the basic bullet points reflecting what has to happen to restore liberty to America:

1. Obtain the moral upper hand regarding the morality of capitalism.

2. Politically disenfranchise and remove the left/progressives from power.

3. Correct the mistaken approaches to liberty of religious conservatives and return individual rights to their proper positions as fundamental principles of society.

4. Change the educational system and teach children logic, the scientific method, rational philosophy and how to determine a proper ethics.

In another chapter, I will write about the importance of opposing altruism and eliminating it as an influence in society. Here, I will comment on point #2 above about removing the left totally from power. In my view, this is the only position we can take. We should not even talk to anyone on the left unless it is to refute their lies and demand that they resign from their positions of power. What today's radicals are doing in advocating coercive government has gone beyond mere disagreement and entered into the realms of deception and corruption.

The basis of this approach can be found in the approaches taken by the world against Nazism. Once the world realized it had an enemy in the Nazis, they knew this enemy had to be smashed completely...and that is exactly what the world did; they ensured that the Germans could never again espouse the kinds of ideas that led to such atrocities.

The Alinsky Radicals are the children of the Weather Underground pretending to be mainstream. They are not nice people; they are killers looking for another way to destroy capitalism.

We have not yet learned the clear lesson about the left. To learn that lesson, we need to understand the moral failure of Marxism and other forms of leftism. Marxist philosophies are not about civilized government; they are an attack on the very idea of civilized government. Marxism is about tyranny. Just like the Nazis, the left today is about the sacrifice of the individual to the collective; and it is this very principle, as instituted by the Nazis, that led to the annihilation of the Jews in Germany and Poland.

As with any corrupt group, they practice a dangerous pragmatism. Likewise, the left is capable of picking up and leveraging any idea that can be used to advance the goal of gaining power. So, a leftist could be a fascist today or a racist tomorrow depending on the political winds. The specific form of government that a given Marxist gang takes (in its rise to power) can be anything that is politically feasible; and at that point any form of government bigotry and coercion can emerge. This is the danger inherent in Marxism: concentration camps and genocide are always the result when groups with like coercive premises vie for power using any means necessary.

Consider that a Marxist state can never achieve long-term economic stability. There is no example in history of a long-standing successful fascist or socialist state. This is because coercive manipulation of the economy always makes things worse. Why would any intelligent group of people advocate such a failed system? Why do the Alinsky Radicals? Why do we allow them to ascend to power?

A coercive government, whether fascist or communist, will

always lie to the people. They will always hide their own culpability for plundering the property of the people. Once a government depends on lying, it will necessarily persecute anyone who does not believe the lies.

Consider that a free people, as long as they are free, can be productive indefinitely. Their energy and work go toward making their lives better and this provides the incentive to keep being productive. When a coercive government begins skimming their production through high taxes and money inflation, the people have to work harder to accomplish the same good standard of living as before. So why even vote for someone who promises re-distribution?

The leftist radicals always lie because they don't want people to understand their ultimate goal which is central government controlled by them. In order to continue their incremental advances toward total control, they will agree with conservatives on some issues today and then disagree on the same issues tomorrow. They must be constantly changing, advocating force and rights at the same time and then only talking about rights at another time. They are chameleons who will say whatever they must in order to stoke whatever prejudices will convince people to let them take the reins of government. Their only principle is that the end justifies the means. Why vote for someone who does not consistently stand on man's rights?

We must be clear; a negotiated peace with the radical leftists, or any kind of stalemate, would not mean a loss on their part. It would mean a win. They will not abandon their plans for national hegemony. They may give in today but tomorrow they'll be back to their old tactics of complaining about systemic problems that they have created. They will be constantly renewing their assaults on freedom and individual rights as long as people are listening. Nothing can stop this political assault except the full and complete decisive victory of individual rights and limited government over totalitarian control.

Toward this goal, it is important to realize that the ideas of the left are dangerous. We must recognize that, no matter what they say, they are not proponents of freedom or the consistent application of the Constitution. They will continue to play "real politick" while attempting to fool us into accepting them as "normal"; and they will continue to propose boondoggle after boondoggle in order to take over our lives. When it is too late for us, only then will they remove the mask of "democracy" and expose the evil totalitarian monster beneath.

This is not the time for a loyal opposition to the Democrats. This is the time for a total repudiation of all positions derived from Marxist premises. Marx is false so any "pragmatic" solution derived from Marx is also false. Whoever does not work for this total repudiation of the left is on the side of the left. We must reject every measure, every idea, every proposed bill, every program, every regulation and every form of re-distribution that is espoused by progressives. We must fight them wholesale in any peaceful way we can so we don't have to fight another revolution that spills blood. It is either the rule of the left or our liberty. If they win, we lose. Let's defeat them now while there is still time.

Toward this purpose, we should recognize that the left dominates our universities. Alinsky Radicals are turning out like-minded progressives by the thousands and these young people are flooding into the professions knowing only the lies they have been taught in school.

Tenure, which is the practice of ensuring a teaching position to a professor who has "earned" it, gives leftists a virtual monopoly in the universities. This causes intellectual stagnation and "political correctness". On the contrary, we need competing ideas, a free, open debate, not the uniformity and regimentation that we find in the universities today. Eliminating tenure will loosen the hold the left has over the minds of our young people.

Educators who have a secular world-view that fosters individual rights must begin to fight the entrenched leftist monopoly in the universities and engage in the hard struggle to compete for the minds of young people. We need more advocates of individual rights in the universities fighting against the Alinsky Radicals head-to-head.

Cultural Marxism

> "Election Day is one day a year and the culture is the other 364 days a year, so if you're not out there competing in the schools, competing in the pop culture, competing in the media, competing in the mainline churches then the air that we breathe becomes liberal; that's the default setting of society and whoever gets elected on a Tuesday morning in November doesn't actually make that much difference."[14]

I define Cultural Marxism as the subconscious infiltration of Marxist ideas into the mainstream of American life. Such ideas function in society, not only as subversive impositions of an alien philosophy but as accepted American premises that drive American culture. Cultural Marxism influences our entertainment, our education, our churches and our politics. It lays the foundations for legislation and holds the power of accepted ideas.

Yet, Marxism is seldom brought forward as part of a distinct ideology. Instead, it is merged with pragmatism as a pseudo-viable philosophy that can be practiced in our daily lives. As pragmatism, Cultural Marxism is put forward as a source for "practical" solutions that have an aura of realism. It smuggles into society unacknowledged Marxist views, and, is not seen as the cause of damage to society. It is a perfect cover for the atrocities of the left.

The process of insinuating Marxism into common issues is pretty simple. The left does it by first complaining about a "problem" that has been created by capitalism and then

[14] Mark Steyn on Fox News "Fox and Friends" October 20, 2014

offering a "practical" solution for solving that problem.

Never mind that the problem was not created by capitalism. In fact, in the overwhelming number of cases, the problem is actually caused by government intervention; in short, by Marxist/progressive ideas. Despite this fact, the Marxist progressives think that more government intervention will solve the problem caused by government intervention. A good example is health care which is burdened by massive government controls that weaken its ability to provide competent health care. To fix these problems, government seeks to impose an even more massive government program that re-distributes medical services and create long lines, poor coverage and rationing of health care.

Yet, progressives continue to blame capitalism for the problems it has created. Don't be surprised that this is what they say to explain the Great Depression in 1929. They declare that it was an unregulated economy that caused the depression when the truth is that it was caused by government banking and tariff policies. And what's even worse, they used the depression as an excuse to create a series of massive boondoggles that wasted the productive energy of the American worker.

One key reason for the dominance of Cultural Marxism is the left's divorcing of Marxist solutions from their Marxist ideological base. This is accomplished by their avoidance of Marxist terminology when arguing for their unworkable "solutions. Marxist proposals are instead presented as practical (pragmatic) solutions whose ends are the collectivist common good. Rather than explicitly advancing Marxist goals, the left pretends to be advancing practical goals that work. Yet, the premises of these "solutions" are always Marxist anti-capitalism, anti-value, anti-mind and anti-liberty.

Where a Marxist in the past would say that capitalism must be eliminated, the Cultural Marxist (as pragmatist) merely advances a government program or regulation that is supposed to fix a flaw in the capitalist system. They even claim that their coercive solutions will create affluence and prosperity and "stimulate" consumer spending. References to Marx or Marxist ideology are avoided in order to attach an aura of practicality to Progressive ideas.

With the words, "workers of the world unite",[15] Karl Marx and Friedrich Engels made the world captive to an elaborate set of lies (Marxism) that they presented as valid philosophy. The real-world consequences of those lies infect our minds and society today. Condensed into various ideas taken as truth, Cultural Marxism causes men to make bad decisions, not only when voting but even in their daily lives.

You can recognize a Cultural Marxist through his anti-capitalism. For instance, unions encourage workers to agitate and fight their capitalist job providers, preferring to portray these men as evil, heartless and exploitative. Attitudes of hatred toward corporations develop across society and create a national division where none is necessary. It forces corporations, beset by lawsuits and onerous regulations to try to influence government in their favor which exacerbates the problem by giving the government a chance to control their activities and extort money from them.

This anti-capitalism also infiltrates our art as it advances works that portray the "plight of the working man" who presumably struggles against a system that degrades, devalues and destroys traditional, pre-capitalist values. Today, leftists don't consider any of this to be Marxist. By their reasoning, it is just the truth and this gives them the

---

[15] Communist Manifesto

opportunity to impose their version of reality upon an unsuspecting citizenry.

Many people listen to politicians who insinuate anti-capitalism into their speeches (Warren, Sanders, et al) and vote for regulations over Wall Street, banks, financial firms and other large companies. Most don't see a Marxist base here. But the key feature of anti-capitalism is that corporations are evil. This is Cultural Marxism.

Professors in universities spout anti-capitalist lies and encourage foreign students in their classrooms to fight against American "domination" in their own countries. The result is oligarchies, fascist states, socialist states and even communist governments intent on converting all industrial property to state property. The result is destruction of property, destruction of commerce, nepotism and genocide. See Venezuela. None of this has anything to do with Marxist premises, it is thought. These are merely valid assessments of international issues. On the contrary, this is Cultural Marxism influencing events around the world.

In the early days of communism, many adherents realized that pure communism would not be accepted because capitalism, limited government and individual rights were firmly established. They argued that the best way of influencing society in the direction of communism was to change the values of the culture by means of a peaceful revolution fought by the intellectuals in the media and universities. Novelists wrote books like "The Jungle" and "The Ugly American" and movie directors made thousands of movies where the villain was a capitalist with unlimited resources trying to take over the world, the neighborhood, the farm or a smaller competitor. No one thought this had anything to do with Karl Marx. Capitalism was evil; it was just a fact, they argued. This is Cultural Marxism and it sent readers and movie goers back home with an attitude that every capitalist, even their own bosses, were crooks.

Since altruism was a powerful moral tool, the Marxists took to using a "moral cover" to get their ideas accepted by the average man. This covered for the Marxist legislative agenda by invoking Jesus, and his exhortations to help the poor and the common man. On this basis, it became easier to advance the ideas of socialism in Europe and "liberalism" in the USA because altruism, helping people, was deemed good. Everybody loved Jesus and everybody loves the common man. No one associated this with the class struggle or with the imposition of socialism. This is Cultural Marxism, and everyone influenced by it became less questioning about the motives of the Cultural Marxists.

When an idea, particularly one that impacts culture, is false, the consequences can be particularly negative. As Dr. Harry Binswanger informs us:

"The first step in judging the validity of an idea is to identify its source: is it based on fact or fantasy? If the idea is evidence-based, one can check the interpretation placed on that evidence; but that which is asserted arbitrarily – proceeding from "what if?" or "why not?" or "it may well be" – offers no evidence to be interpreted. Such ideas are not in the realm of logic but of make-believe."[16]

The advocacy of Marxism in the form of pragmatism is indeed, based upon "make-believe", fully false and totally without merit. Its influence on our culture has let loose predatory, dictatorial and very bad people who are turning

[16] Dr. Harry Binswanger, How We Know – Epistemology on an Objectivist Foundation, hardcover, TOF Publications, P292

lives upside down. These people are "killers" in the full meaning of the word. They kill people by means of their view of reality, their view of the nature of man and the nature of a proper society. These ideas and these "killers" should be removed from power and their influence completely eradicated. The place to start is by exposing the evil of Cultural Marxism.

Hegel

In the Introduction to this book, I mentioned that I was not providing a complete history of the progressive movement. I do not need to refute every point made by the anti-capitalist Cultural Marxists if I can refute the one key premise upon which their philosophy is built.

This premise is derived from the work of Georg Hegel (1770 - 1831) who had a profound influence on Marx. Early in life, Karl Marx studied at the University of Berlin where Hegel had taught. At this point in time, Hegel's ideas were gaining broad acceptance throughout Germany and the world. Students wanted to participate in the new philosophy that was turning the world upside down.

For Hegel, reality was a state of consciousness that can only know the world it creates. According to this (circular) view, there is no reality independent of consciousness. What we call reality or existence is something in consciousness, something non-material and a product of whatever consciousness created it.

Reality, for Hegel, was not the product of any particular mind but of one Absolute Mind[17]. This Absolute Mind is intent on manifesting itself, on "realizing" itself by moving through various stages of development (and here we see where Marx got his idea of the historical class struggle moving inexorably toward the collapse of capitalism). Hegel proclaimed that thesis, anti-thesis and synthesis were stages of history representing the Absolute Mind's progress toward full self-realization. We are all just passing each other in the night of this Absolute Mind, fully meaningless and mere cogs in the

---

[17] For early sources of this concept, see Anaxagoras, Plato (Timaeus) and Aristotle's Immovable Mover.

wheel so to speak.

Hegel thought that his dialectical process actually involved the real world. We humans could understand how the Absolute Mind brought order to the world by using the same dialectical method of thesis, anti-thesis and synthesis. His Speculative Reasoning brought with it what he considered to be a strict logic that could help us deduce important truths and understand the exact relation between the Absolute Mind and the real world.

Luke Mastin tells us:

"Hegel's main philosophical project, then, was to take the contradictions and tensions he saw throughout modern philosophy, culture and society, and interpret them as part of a comprehensive, evolving, rational unity that, in different contexts, he called "the absolute idea" or "absolute knowledge". He believed that everything was interrelated and that the separation of reality into discrete parts (as all philosophers since Aristotle had done) was wrong. He advocated a kind of historically-minded Absolute Idealism (developed out of the Transcendental Idealism of Immanuel Kant), in which the universe would realize its spiritual potential through the development of human society, and in which mind and nature can be seen as two abstractions of one indivisible whole Spirit."[18]

Hegel has developed an invalid metaphysical principle and applied it to the entirety of reality while consigning it to the status of a creation of consciousness. That is a massive (circular) re-organization of reality – actually a new invention of a new reality that does not exist.

---

[18] http://www.philosophybasics.com/philosophers_hegel.html

If every idea of the Absolute (thesis) has within it its opposite (anti-thesis) and if the Absolute Mind creates reality (synthesis), then every metaphysical concrete has within it a contradiction that must then be resolved by the Absolute Mind as it moves to a higher stage of its own development. Never mind that Hegel merely postulates this metaphysic (and the inner contradiction) without validation; the flaw in this line of thinking is that only Hegel's wishing makes it so. As it was with Anaxagoras, the source of Hegel's ideas, there was no way to actually connect this mind to the creation of any reality.

Needless to say, this unprovable assertion is an indication of the philosophical corruption that Hegel bequeathed to Marx and Engels. Not only does Hegel claim to be describing the world that *Mind* created, he is also falsely asserting a metaphysical principle that is independent of Mind (that yielded disastrous results when an economic motive was asserted by Marx and Engels).

To state that reality (created by the mind) has an inner contradiction means that there are two realities; a reality and an anti-reality. Yet, if there is an Absolute Mind there must also be an Anti-Absolute Mind with each stage. The Absolute Mind cannot "develop" without this contradiction of a contradiction.

If there is a Hegel, there must also be an anti-Hegel. But this gets us nowhere. Further, when Marx postulated that history moved by an amended historical process of his own wishful thinking; and that the key to his anti-version of historical development was economic class; the result could only be a materialistic reality that operated according to arbitrary and unrealistic processes (remember the Mises quote). If this historical process holds that we are always defending the economic class into which we are born, then wasn't Marx also defending the economic class into which he was born? But which class was that? He was born into a period of emerging capitalist dominance still partly mired in the feudal system.

Within this context, any contradiction you advance is an epistemological one pretending to be metaphysical; this makes Hegel's (and Marx's) metaphysics a contradiction of itself. By Hegel's view, he should say that every concept has an inner contradiction.

Yet, Hegel's concept of "being" is essentially without content, designating nothing. One cannot have a metaphysical world created by epistemology. Concept formation and knowledge can only refer to an existing world; can only be about an existing world. In Hegel's sense, "being" is an obscure term used to designate a non-existent that can then be epistemologically (magically) infused with its exact opposite; which makes it bereft of content, completely arbitrary and completely Hegel and not Hegel.

An indefinite "something" used as a fundamental concept can be infused with anything that Hegel decides. This false method, needless to say, has nothing to do with reality and how the real world works. For Hegel, there is no such real world, except the world that he, Hegel, makes (consider that this applies to Marx and Engels also).

Let's get back to sanity. Reality is comprised of entities that exist independently of the mind. They have only the characteristics they have and nothing else. There is no opposing content within them. They are what they are, and it is the purpose of man's mind to identify the nature of what exists.

Since Hegel is only talking about, for want of a better word, Platonic essences, and since the essences are a product of a consciousness (his consciousness), there is no way that Hegel's interpretation can represent anything but his own blind desire to come up with a universe that is opposed to all of existence; in the name of existence.

In order to sound plausible, Hegel relied on the principle of change, the old Heraclitan saw. He postulated an amazing idea that almost worked: for Hegel, change is the concept that resolves the conflict between being (thesis) and non-being (anti-thesis). The problem was that change cannot resolve a conflict between what something is and what Hegel says is its opposite. In fact, nothing has its own opposite within it.

What is "change" and how does it handle the positive and the contradictory within itself? Does it have its own opposite within it? Anti-change? How would that work? And how are we to know anything when everything is an invention of an Absolute Mind? Hegel has created a subjectivist cornucopia and a collective death wish.

There is no proof of the Absolute Mind's creation of being. There is no proof or validation of the Absolute Mind; it is merely a creation of man's mind based in mysticism. Nor is the Absolute Mind an axiomatic concept. This idea is actually a way for a secular philosopher to imply the existence of an Almighty God.

The fact that change happens is not enough to explain a materialistic world. In fact, a better description of this process in the real world is the concept of cause and effect not some mystical Hegelian concept of "being versus anti-being". What things change into cannot be thought into existence; change happens to things because of their natures as specific entities.

The real question is change to what and how? Hegel's answer is pure unprovable speculation.

For Hegel, the assumption that change reconciles a contradiction cannot mean that he is able to identify what change will actually do. And that is the heart of the matter. When he promises to know the path that the Absolute Mind will travel, he is merely speculating, guessing and inventing out of whole cloth. How does he know that change always brings about a reconciliation of the contradictory? What if, instead, it brings about a contrary or something entirely different that Hegel has no way of predicting?

In fact, history refutes Hegel's and Marx's predictions about history. Many of the anti-theses they postulate do not come about in history. For instance, after many decades of predicting the victory of socialism, socialism has yet to replace capitalism. In fact, we have many decades of socialists trying to make socialism the victor over capitalism while also killing many capitalists in the process.

This makes their ideas arbitrary constructs that have nothing to do with how the real world (or the Absolute Mind) works. There is no "connection", no "necessity" as Hume might say (in a different context). You can only get necessity by means of cause and effect and a mere concept such as thesis and anti-thesis limits the full range of possibilities for the Hegelians and this consigns dialectic to the unpredictable (or the not likely).

Indeed, Hegel's theories have no predictive value, and this applies to Marx and his assumption that economic classes are the preeminent categories that result in historical change. It does not follow that capitalism contains its own contradiction and that socialism is the result of synthesis (or even that synthesis takes place).

What is "synthesis" and how does it work and how can we prove that it has happened as described by Hegel or Marx? We can't. We can only analyze the natures of economic systems and identify the features of each; then determine which system is the best. Then we choose the system we would like to establish. There is no miracle that replaces capitalism with socialism. Moving from capitalism to socialism is a moral judgment made by individuals not by some Absolute Mind or anti-Absolute Mind. If men try socialism and find that it produces none of the benefits of capitalism, then they should make the appropriate change which is to re-establish capitalism.

What they would learn, if they are logical, is that capitalism is based upon freedom of the individual and socialism is based upon state ownership of the individual. One cannot say that force is superior to freedom as a universal historical premise. It has never been proven that force brings good economic conditions or that capitalism is a failed system.

If socialism is superior to capitalism, then that superiority must be based on something; fundamental facts about the two systems. A system that is freer than capitalism (but there is no such system); or that is based upon a more "perfect" freedom than is hitherto defined (Marx's arguments on this issue notwithstanding) can only be a myth or contradiction.

An economic or social system must derive from the fundamental principles that make it up; not from history. A truly superior economic system must derive from the principles that make up capitalism, not from the contradictory of freedom.

It is the fact of individual rights that characterizes capitalism. What then is anti-capitalism but anti-individual rights? We know now that anti-individual rights creates dictatorship (see the 20th century). In truth, there is no mystical or materialistic movement of history that rules these systems; there is only right or wrong; ethics and choosing one of these systems is not a matter of history but of human (value) choice. We choose the system we get. We get the system we choose. History is not a magical device that gives it to us. Marx is totally wrong.

As Mises correctly observes, Hegelian dialectic is "a system easy of abuse by those who seek to dominate thought by arbitrary flights of fancy and metaphysical verbosity..." As a foundation for Marxism, then, Hegelian dialectic is a bust.

If we follow this, we realize that Marx predicted nothing, and that Marxism is a farce as both philosophy and economic critique. In other words, violent revolution, or even progressivism, the slow steady march of coercion via pragmatism, are not going to lead to a dream called social justice. There is nothing in Marxism that is logical or even scientific. Indeed, there is nothing to Marxism except arbitrary and blind foolish speculation.

There is no guarantee that, in reality, concepts will behave in a way that Hegelian and Marxist philosophers project. Few thinkers that I am aware of have even tried to suggest that there is no reason to believe that entities have within them their opposites (anti-theses). This is because concepts, when correctly derived, do not come from metaphysics; they come from the mind as it ascertains reality; from epistemology as it focuses on metaphysics.

A concept (such as socialism) does not represent a magical entity that rules reality; such a concept is a product of man's thinking as he apprehends the real world. It has no ability to control what happens in the real world. This applies even to concepts supposedly invented by a non-existent Absolute Mind (they came as fantasies from a man's mind). Merely stating that the concept "being" has a contradiction, non-being, does not guarantee that this is so. It may sound good, and feel good to some, but there is no reason to believe that it operates as it is thought by some; no reason to believe that it leads to any form of utopian society.

We can therefore conclude:

- Neither entities nor concepts can be contradictory in nature. A thing is what it is and only what it is. All entities in existence have some form and some state. Concepts are man-made and exist in the mind as useful tools that help in ascertaining reality (if they are properly conceived). It is man's responsibility to organize his conceptual material so it corresponds to existence.
- There is no reason to believe that there is any such thing as a materialistic historical process. Concepts do not move history. Man defines concepts by looking at reality but the concepts themselves only exist in the mind. Hegel's methodology is flawed and incompetent and can rightly be classified as pure mysticism.
- When Marx uses a variant of Hegel's methodology to try to predict the next phase of economic dialectic, he is engaged in a false quest. There is no way for him to predict what will happen in the future by this means. Socialism is nothing more than a return to the repressive systems of the past and not an inevitable product of some future new system.
- Because the next phase of Marx's economic development did not come about on its own, as Marx had predicted, Marx had to preach violent revolution by the proletariat against the capitalist. In fact, both the "proletariat" and the capitalist

have continued to flourish despite the mixed systems that resulted from Marxist and progressive interventionism.

- There is no validity to the idea that the process of thesis, anti-thesis and synthesis is a metaphysical or epistemological principle that applies across the universe. There is no reason to think that a "thing" or "concept" has within it its exact opposite. Things change. They change from something to something according to the principles of physics and cause and effect. Rationalism, the idea that concepts determine reality, is a false quest.

- There is no validity to the idea that the real world was created by an Absolute Mind. Dialectic idealism is as invalid as Plato's essences.

- Hegel's collectivism and state worship are arbitrary and invalid.

- The constant Marxist criticisms of profit and capitalism are corrupt – the anti-profit and anti-dissent collectivist attitudes of the Marxists are all false assertions. Altruism, the requirement of duty or sacrifice, is also a false assertion that has no role in human moral living. Altruism is the cause of human sacrifice and genocide.

As Tismaneanu informs us:

"With characteristic nineteenth-century hubris, Marx declared his social theory the ultimate scientific formula, as exact and precise as the algorithms of mathematics or the demonstrations of formal logic. Not to recognize their validity was for Marx, as for his successors, evidence of historical blindness, ideological bias, or "false consciousness," which were characteristic of those who opposed Marxist solutions to social questions. Prisoners of the bourgeois mentality, alienated victims of ideological mystifications, and non-Marxist theorists—all purveyors of false consciousness—were scorned and dismissed as supporters of the status quo. At the opposite pole, the proletarian viewpoint, celebrated by Marx and crystallized in the form of historical materialism, was thought to provide ultimate knowledge and the recipe for universal happiness."[19]

"For Marx, communism united ideological superiority, political militancy, and an unflinching and resolute appreciation of historical tasks."[20] ...all of which were balderdash.

But is this what the world wanted; a massive historical war of destruction, deception; a turning of everything upside down? Did the world really find oppression in capitalism or was the charge of oppression something invented in order to justify expropriation and murder by anti-capitalists? Did communists really want a better world or were they merely "real politick" expropriators, gangsters seeking to replace a republican form of government with a totalitarian one? Yes, absolutely.

Marxism engages in a perennial struggle to excise what it considers capitalism's evil while at the same time trying to remain viable as a cultural ethic. This Marxist cultural ethic, the means by which it professes to pursue the good, freedom, democracy and liberation of the downtrodden, is a lie that no honest person should want to propagate. Marxists are not merely good people seeking to install human benevolence. On the contrary, Marxism is an economic philosophy related to the march of nihilism in society, the desire to destroy human values and honest living.

With every failure of Marxism to produce abundance, every incident of ethnic or class genocide, every descent into mass murder, Marxists insist that those negatives do not represent

---

[19] The Devil in History by Vladimir Tismaneanu, University of California Press, P. 164
[20] Ibid, Page 169

"true" Marxism. They'll get it right the next time, they tell us. After all, there is something "magical" about the idea of helping the poor; there is a better, more peaceful result just around the corner if we stick with it and refuse to let reality intervene.

How does Marxism retain its magical aspects? What makes it transcend its negatives and continue to arise every few generations with its promise of social justice and utopian freedom? This can only be done by means of intellectual deception, by teaching each new generation that the old Marxism was not really Marxism and that the new Marxism is the magic formula. This time, they tell us, they won't kill a bunch of people while they continue getting rid of the remaining elements of capitalism; by killing a bunch of people.

For some reason, the Marxists are intent upon judging the tenets of Marxism by their good intentions rather than their criminality. Yet, it is their criminality that disenfranchises the productive, proclaims selfishness as evil and denigrates the idea of capital investment by a few greedy fat cats.

"The characteristically paranoid perception of the world as an arena of deadly hostilities being conducted conspiratorially by an insidious and implacable enemy against the self finds highly systematized expression in terms of political and ideological symbols that are widely understood and accepted in the given social milieu. Through a special and radical form of displacement of private affects upon public objects, this world-image is politicized. In the resulting vision of reality, both attacker and intended victim are projected on the scale of large human collectives."[21]

---

[21] The Soviet Political Mind by Robert C. Tucker

To be clear, this means that Marx was wrong and his collectivist followers such as Bill Ayers, Reverend Wright, Barack Obama and Bernie Sanders are wrong too. There is no such thing as historical materialism. Not only does it not exist, even when men dedicate their lives to it in brutal violence or even gradual violence, it will not lead to a better world. It will only extend the reign of violence and deceit to the detriment of people whose lives are exploited by false premises.

The idea that we can understand reality or history by logical deduction from floating abstractions alone is problematic. There is no substitute for looking at reality and identifying how things work. There is no substitute for free people judging values for themselves and living according to the pursuit of those values. There is no substitute for a productive purpose advanced by a free individual. The idea that you can deduce everything from a "foundational" principle disconnected from reality ignores the fact that reality will not bend to anyone's or Anything's wish. Rather, ala Bacon, reality must be apprehended in order to be obeyed.

Any philosophy that is based upon floating abstractions such as altruism and a fictitious historical conflict, must necessarily create cognitive failures on the part of individuals and specifically in the minds of their founders. The judgments of these founders necessarily lead people to decisions that negatively affect their lives. This is what happens to every individual influenced by Marx's principles on economic and political issues.

To assert that reality is all about a class struggle and then to insinuate that class struggle into one's understanding of reality can only produce strife. This is what is wrong with Marxism and this makes it an evil philosophy, a pseudo-philosophy based upon pseudo-science, pseudo-morality and pseudo-politics. The one thing we can be sure of is that the wars and social conflict created by Marxism are real. That is Cultural Marxism and you are its victim.

Altruism

People who advocate altruism as a moral principle should take note: Societies based upon altruism always fail. This is because altruism destroys human value and, as a consequence, it destroys the incentive or ability of people to create human value. This means that altruism is destructive of human life.

Yet, in every study of such societies, whether by economists or political philosophers, altruism is always ignored as a factor in their failures. It is as if this non-principle has nothing to do with anything; as if it is completely blameless of any wrongs done in its name.

Some people ask how altruism could ever be responsible for the collapse of Nazi Germany or the Soviet Union or Cuba or Venezuela or Cambodia or…? Everyone "knows" that altruism is about benign concern for others. It is about helping others. Isn't that a good thing? How could it be responsible for killer societies?

Altruism has come down to us as a moral precept accepted without question. Altruism supposedly validates the need for individual sacrifice imposed by a government seeking to help the poor. Altruism supposedly makes things better for all of us. Of course, it is true that people like Stalin and Hitler preached sacrifice for the collective and did atrocious things in the name of altruism.

Altruism is the core premise of people who advocate the coercive, re-distributive state. Isn't altruism the premise of those who take from one man and give to another? Indeed, altruism means, at base, "otherism", the idea that others are more important than the individual. Altruism is at the core of any social system that fosters intervention by government into the life of the individual. Governments oppress people in the name of sacrifice for the collective in the name of altruism.

Altruism can be practiced privately, without force, as well as publicly; instituted by a government. Yet, regardless of whether people sacrifice voluntarily or under duress, the result of altruism is the same in either case: the individual gives up values that he worked to achieve.

This is the key to understanding altruism; any time you give up a value, you are violating your personal hierarchy of values (your chosen code of values). If your mother tells you to do at least one thing every day for someone else, to the extent that you do it, you are kept from benefiting yourself, pleasing yourself, elevating your mind or improving your life; that is a sacrifice and your mother is doing you a disservice. You are losing the possibility of bringing values into your life because of those sacrifices.

Every act of altruism, is, at base, a sacrifice of your mind. You need your mind in order to decide what is proper for you. You need your mind to begin the process of thinking; the very act of telling yourself to focus is a volitional act. When you use your mind to advance your values, you are living rationally, and you learn that consistent rationality means consistently living for your values. It could get you killed if some altruist (such as Stalin) decides it is time for you to sacrifice your life for the sake of a meaningless war or re-distribution program (slave labor).

On the other hand, any act that takes from you the product of your thinking and gives it to someone else is a violation of the integrity of your moral code and it harms your ability to consistently live for your values.

The key is not merely being free to choose and pursue your values but being able to do it consistently and volitionally. This means you must also value your mind. If you know how important it is to your survival, if you cherish and love the use of your mind and know how critical it is to your success; you will feel a shudder of revulsion when you are told to give up what you struggled to create, and you will consider the suggestion of sacrifice to be evil to the core. You will treat it as equivalent to the suggestion that you die – for it is, indeed, an attack on you.

In every altruist transfer of value, one individual must give up his life, mind, time and/or possessions for the sake of someone else. Because it harms the valuer, the producer of values, the act of taking that value is immoral. Even if the giver is vastly rich and barely notices the loss, altruism assumes that he is guilty by nature and must sacrifice whether he agrees with it or not. This is an attack on the value of the mind.

To understand this, we must learn what values are and why keeping one's values is important for you. First of all, values are intellectual products before they can be physical products. An individual must conceive, identify or discover his values and understand their importance for his life. This means that your values could not exist without your deciding upon them. The person who receives those values without effort did not make the decision to produce those values; you, the productive individual made that decision. They are yours; nobody else's. As Ayn Rand has said, "The concept of 'value' is not a primary; it presupposes an answer to the questions: of value to *whom* and for *what*?"[22]

_____

[22] The Virtue of Selfishness by Ayn Rand, iBooks ebook, *"The Objectivist Ethics"*

Your code of values represents a singular unit, a concept that integrates your actions around a specific life-purpose. It is not something that comes willy nilly, disconnected from your life and of little import. It is of life and death importance. In a sense, if you give up one small value, you are giving up your life because that value is part of the whole without which the whole cannot be accomplished in the manner you intended. To sacrifice part of the whole is to delay or frustrate your accomplishment of your singular purpose in life. This is no small matter regardless of how much the altruists want you to think it is.

A value is something you worked to acquire; something you thought beneficial to your life. Now you are told to give it up and not to reap the benefit that you had wanted to experience. Yet, you chose that value and spent the time and energy necessary for pursuing it. Whether the value is a nice car or a pack of chewing gum, it means something to you. When you are told to give it up, you are never asked if you deserve to keep it; you must give it up even if you need it for survival.

Consider what it means to have your child's last meal sitting in front of him or her and then having someone come in and take it because someone else is hungry. That would be altruism. That would be a sacrifice of your child for the sake of someone else.

Today, with the convenience and utility that money brings, you don't have to give up your chewing gum. You merely give up money. But money still represents values that you earned. It represents your next car, a refrigerator or a tire that will keep you safe on the highway. You may even be taking food out of your child's mouth.

Yet, the person who is demanding your money for the poor

thinks you shouldn't keep it for your own selfish gain. He thinks it is moral to point a (government) gun at you and take it. By forcing you to sacrifice, he is also forcing you to defer the purchase of your values when you need them. Will anyone know that you and your children died because you could not purchase a new tire? Remember the question, "of value to whom and for what?" What gives someone else the superior intelligence that enables him to know how you should spend your money? The only answer is that he has the gun and you don't.

So, let's look at the "for what" part of this equation. The first thing you notice is that the person collecting the money from you (voluntarily or forcibly) must take some of it for himself so he can live. The only thing he does in life is go around collecting peoples' money; he produces nothing but a full collection basket. All of it, including the basket, was made by someone else; not by him. Remember, this is your value that you created with your mind and energy and now he is taking it so he can buy values for himself before he even helps anyone else with what is left.

He may not want you to know that the beat up old car he is driving is for show. Back in his garage, he has a shiny new sports car that he drives on weekends when he's not collecting your money.

You can also be sure that when he hands the money over to his friend, the needy person, he, the collector, is getting credit for helping the needy, not you. You are already forgotten. You are part of what I call "the unseen". There is your "for what" another attack on your mind.

Now you must ask yourself, does he really deserve that sports car? Well, what did he create? Did he work in a factory that created something of value to trade (value for value) with others? No, he took your money that you earned and now he has a better life than you. All he did was take your money and give it to himself with a little bit of it left over for the other guy.

Remember, he promised you that he would be transferring your "donation" to some needy person. Let's look at this needy person's "for what?" One thing is clear, since this person did not work for the value you created, he does not really care about it nor does he want it. Or, he may want it, but knows that all he needs to do is declare himself needy and someone will give him what you worked for.

This person may be a low-skilled individual who earns less than you because he quit school without graduating. If he became employed for a time, he may not have liked it so he got himself fired and went on welfare. He may have a nicer home than you and, overall, a higher income too. After all, he's getting many donations while you are only getting your own donation.

It is also possible that the person getting your money may be extremely rich. He could own a company working government contracts. He got these contracts by spending your money, in the form of a government grant, partying with a government official who agreed to give him millions of dollars in contracts. Your money has also helped him pay a politician to write legislation for his industry that drives away competition. Or he could be making something so worthless, like solar panels, that once they are purchased by the government (with your money again) no one else wants them. How's that for a "for what"?

Now, let's ask the question again, "of value to whom and for what?" Considering all this, these people did not work for the money you worked for. They don't value that money. In fact, they think they are entitled to your money because they have clever lawyers or good politician friends or nice welfare advisors and community organizers. There is always someone somewhere who creates absolutely no value of any kind and receives millions of dollars helping other people get and spend your money - and they care nothing about you and what you did to make that money. Also, they don't care about receiving quality or paying a fair price for what they buy with your money.

Of course, there is a litany of talking points the altruists have cooked up to make you feel guilty for making your money. If they can convince you that your mind, your work, your time and your life are meaningless and valueless, they can make you feel guilty so you will give everything you have earned away.

The "self-appointed moral authority" who takes your money is adept at finding people who need help. Usually, whatever happens to a "needy" person is taken as a major emergency that must be solved by "us".

Needless to say, the only possible solution is for "us" (notice how collectivism always creeps in when altruism is afoot) to pool our money and solve this person's problems. Forget that we must all sacrifice in order to correct this emergency. To refuse to help this person is cruel. Forget, that the free market has a range of solutions; the one overriding truth is that this person is suffering, and "we" must eliminate his suffering by getting together to solve the problem.

What usually happens in such situations? Almost always, when left to his own devices, the "needy" individual solves his own problem. The emergency-monger who has asked for contributions is left standing while holding someone else's money and needing to do nothing after all.

In other cases, someone responds to the emergency by sacrificing his own time or money to solve the problem. This person decides to be the "suffering savior" and make everything all good. For the "self-appointed moral authority" this act validates everything he has been doing in helping the "needy" person. He has "proven" that sacrifice works and that the act of sacrifice is a practical solution. He takes credit for solving the problem while also ignoring the fact that someone else has lost his values.

Needless to say, the voluntary savior gains great praise for his heroic act of self-sacrifice. He is now a great man; someone who is always willing to help others, to give back, to prove that altruism is practical. Everyone is happy, of course, except the "needy" person who is not happy that he is still struggling despite all the help.

But the problem is not solved completely. We still need a few scapegoats to parade as a warning to those who refused to sacrifice when called upon. There is always someone who should have done something but did not. This might be someone who has a little more money than others or someone who is more closely related to the needy; essentially someone who "should" have stepped up and done something but did not. This person is now a pariah, someone who doesn't believe in "giving back". In short, this person is selfish. The amount of vitriol this person experiences, the ostracism and the "singling out" is often so intense that he or she tells the whole "crew" to bug off.

Indeed, the fact that there are so many selfish people around who keep gumming up the works of altruistic self-sacrifice needs to be dealt with. According to the altruists, the progressives and the socialists, we must prevent people from being selfish in the future. The solution is to create a fund (through government) that would pay for any losses by the needy. Make everyone pay a "fair" tax and then whenever someone has a problem that qualifies, he can merely fill out a form and request assistance from government. Needless to say, it would be best if the person chosen to manage this new program was someone we could trust to have the best interest of the needy in mind. Of course, it would be the person who came up with the idea; the "self-appointed moral authority, progressive or socialist". Let's start a new program called the Green New Deal and create massive spending programs that will drain the entire economy.

Yet, even this does not solve the problem. Certainly, lots of money is collected for the fund; but anyone who wants assistance must first prove that he or she is "needy". If a person is working, he or she does not qualify. If a person has money in a savings account, he or she does not qualify. One must be truly poor in order to be served. One must be totally worthless.

The "self-appointed moral authority" is seen as a wonderful person for all the "collective" good he does. Few notice the damage left in his wake, but they do notice that he stirs things up, finds villains everywhere and does his best to make life uncomfortable for the selfish ones who are just trying to survive. What we don't see are the many people who are brought to the brink of destitution by the "call to sacrifice".

The destruction of values is the terrible essence of altruism. Few notice the bodies lying in the ditch; they only notice that someone now has something for which he or she didn't have to pay.

Indeed, the "self-appointed moral authorities" of the world have been at it for millennia and they know just how to push your buttons. For instance, they might say, "Sure there is some waste in government. But we should think about the little child who doesn't have a meal today." Or they might say, "We must look at the loss of self-esteem of children who wear hand-me-down clothes." They will give you hundreds of sob stories, most of which aren't true, to make you feel guilty for not solving someone else's problem by means of making your own life more difficult.

If you respond, "Well, I think those real hard-luck cases are rare in a free society and they could be handled by voluntary giving. I don't want my money sent to fat cats or lazy bums who don't want to work." Their answer: "How can people be so heartless, how can people be so cruel. Easy to be cold, easy to say 'No'".

The truth is that your money is yours – and it should be spent in a way consistent with your values, not contrary to them. Your values are your values. You cannot attain them if a huge part of your paycheck is being squandered. Your money represents your effort to survive to the best of your ability; no more, no less. Why should you limit yourself?

I find it offensive to hear leftists say they have "no problem" "investing" your money. My angry answer is: "Your spending of my money is not the same as my investing it. The fact that you have "no problem" spending it makes you *my* problem. You don't own my money. What gives you the right to spend it? Only a gun; only the false idea that force against free people is proper in society."

The fact that both progressives and conservatives advocate altruism is telling. The only real difference between the two is that progressives are more consistent in their use of force while the conservatives claim an economic argument for not doing it as consistently. This means that the conservatives are compromisers who only haggle about the means and the unintended consequences. They still foster the same impossible end; utopia. That is why they lose elections.

The progressives are only doing the logical thing in a climate where profits are considered evil. They claim that conservative dissenters are merely defending their economic status. This forces conservatives to avoid using their own weak economic arguments. Their only option, to prove they care about the poor, is to vote for the progressives' new programs.

According to politicians, both progressive and conservative, there is supposed to be something primordial and magical about sacrifice. It is deemed "good" by the gods. It represents a universal principle that men have honored for millennia. It brings an aura of goodness to the self-sacrificial man; it breeds respect, self-confidence and high status. A man who gives to others is an advocate of universal progress, social justice and correcting the imbalance of nature.

On the other hand, men who have earned large sums throughout their lives are considered selfish, predatory, materialistic and putting profits over people. At the end of their lives, they give everything away to charity to prove they are not evil. In some circles, they are thought to be buying their way into heaven.

I think the acts of wealthy people giving away their wealth are indeed based upon guilt. Yet it is a guilt imposed by the culture. The guilt is unearned. A wealthy man like Bill Gates did not get wealthy by cheating people. He developed a product so good that it saved people countless hours and helped them earn thousands of dollars. The benefits and savings he helped create have done much more good in the world than virtually all of the money given away by all the philanthropists in the history of the world, Gates included.

Additionally, giving money away to charitable organizations merely wastes that money. Most of it is spent and destroyed by the purchase of consumer goods. If Bill Gates were to take that same money and put it into an investment of some kind, the money would not only come back to him but also create thousands of jobs in the economy through lending to new businesses. As I wrote before, spending is not investing. Money spent cannot come back to the spender. Gates would do the world much more "good", and create much more value (while saving many more lives), if he merely kept his money in a bank.

When altruists criticize selfishness and greed, their goal is to invoke guilt in people and motivate them to give their money away. This short-sighted goal only serves to undercut and discredit the concept which is the real savior of mankind which is rational self-interest. For instance, no one told Obama's minions they were unhappy because they were too selfish. Instead their poor living conditions were the fault of people who were not playing by the rules. Their refusal to do things "for themselves", their willingness to limit themselves, their sloppy thinking, could do nothing but lower their productive skills and their expectations. Obama didn't tell them to raise themselves up because that would undermine his message that sacrifice, not rational selfishness, made America great.

Ayn Rand campaigned for decades about the horrors of altruism. Her novel, Atlas Shrugged, exposed the corruption of altruism as it was expressed through government actions and collective goals. The novel clearly shows, as if it were prophesy, that government interventions are nothing more than the machinations of corrupt politicians trying to become wealthy on the backs of productive citizens. The following quote makes her view clear:

"...there are two questions in ethics, which the traditional moralists lump together into an undifferentiated package-deal — a. What are values? — b. Who should be the beneficiary of values? Since all values have to be gained and/or kept by men's actions, any breach between actor and beneficiary necessitates injustice: the sacrifice of some men to others, of the actors or producers to the beneficiaries. Nothing could ever justify or validate such a breach. Therefore, the Objectivist ethics holds that the actor must always be the beneficiary of the action — that man must act for his own self-interest — but that this right is derived from the nature of values and the nature of man, and, therefore, is applicable only in the context of a rational, objectively demonstrated and validated code of moral values, which determines man's rational self-interest."[23]

If you wanted to encapsulate into one statement the meaning of altruism it would be that popularized by Karl Marx: "**From each according to his ability, to each according to his needs!**" This statement should be the one statement that all pro-liberty advocates should tie around the necks of the Alinsky Radicals and all progressives. These groups could not and would not exist were it not for the foundational role this statement has played in creating their missions and in justifying their means.

---

[23] The Letters of Ayn Rand Letters To A Philosopher

As I have said, altruism is an attack on the human mind, on the makers, the thinkers, the doers and the best among us. Once you dismiss the human mind, you are destroying the source of human values and by default, you are destroying human benevolence. Altruism therefore destroys all actors, givers, middlemen and takers – wholesale. This is why altruism has failed every time it has been tried. This is why genocide and mass murder have often marked the end of societies based upon altruism.

When someone says that the Marxist moral premise ("from each according to his ability…") is correct and that no one should disagree with it, the best statement any "real" man can make is "I don't agree with such evil" and refuse to participate.

The love of altruism and self-sacrifice was recently voiced when the Christian CEO of a company in the USA decided to pay all his employees an equal wage regardless of each individual's productive value to the company. He felt that this was the Christian thing to do. The first people to leave the company were the managers who knew the true value of their work and the impact their minds were having on the profits of the company. Others spoke up saying this action was unfair to the people who worked hardest because it was paying the same salary to people who contributed little to the company. Eventually, this company will either pay each employee according to his results or it will go out of business.

Altruism is evil despite the "good press" it has gotten through the centuries. My book, "The History of Altruism"[24] discusses why this is true. Here, I will simply state that the Alinsky Radicals use altruism as a gimmick; as a way of shaming

---

[24] https://amzn.to/2NR8Sb8

honest people and stealing their production. This theft will take its ultimate form; the mask of hatred will fall, and they will be exposed when the American people realize that freedom is anti-altruism and altruism is anti-freedom.

Anti-"Rules for Radicals"

I've always hesitated to buy books by my philosophical enemies because I don't want to support the publishers who bring us lies. Yet, I understand the importance of understanding your intellectual opponents as thoroughly as possible. This applies especially to progressives who publish books and produce movies full of Marxist anti-capitalism. In fact, I know enough about what they think to see that they are liars and propagandists for a philosophy that I abhor.

To begin my studies of the Alinsky Radicals, I settled for an Adobe Acrobat document that I found on the Internet. It provided the exact information I sought. It is called "Alinsky's Rules for Radicals" By Craig Miyamoto. This short work provided a good background for the Alinsky Radicals and discussed their rules for agitation in American society.

Using this document as foundation, I'm going to provide the best antidote for each rule, the Anti-Rules for Radicals, so to speak. You will find these "Anti-rules" following the words "My comment" after each Alinsky rule. We start with the following from the article:

"Known as the "father of modern American radicalism," Saul D. Alinsky (1909-1972) developed strategies and tactics that take the enormous, unfocused emotional energy of grassroots groups and transform it into effective anti-government and anti-corporate activism. Activist organizations teach his ideas widely taught today as a set of model behaviors, and they use these principles to create an emotional commitment to victory - no matter what.

"Grassroots pressure on large organizations is reality, and there is every indication that it will grow. Because the conflicts manifest in high-profile public debate and often panicked decision-making, studying Alinsky's rules will help organizations develop counteractive strategies that can level the playing field.

"Governments and corporations have inherent weaknesses. And, time and again, they repeat mistakes that other large organizations have made, even repeating their OWN mistakes. Alinsky's out-of-print book - "Rules for Radicals" - illustrates why opposition groups take on large organizations with utter glee, and why these governments and corporations fail to win.

"Large organizations have learned to stonewall and not empower activists. In other words, they try to ignore radical activists and are never as committed to victory as their opposition is committed to defeating them. Result? They are unprepared for the hailstorm of brutal tactics that severely damage their reputation and send them running with their tails between their legs.

"Some of these rules are ruthless, but they work. Here are the rules to be aware of:"

RULE 1: "'Power is not only what you have, but what the enemy thinks you have.' Power is derived from 2 main sources - money and people. "Have-Nots" must build power from flesh and blood. (These are two things of which there is a plentiful supply. Government and corporations always have a difficult time appealing to people, and usually do so almost exclusively with economic arguments.)"

My comment: Anti-rule #1. The first thing is to realize that radicals like the Alinskyites need followers who have little grasp of intellectual topics. They prefer to work with people who can be provided an intellectual base that is easy to believe and explain. They give them the Marxist class struggle and teach them to believe that the American capitalist is a white racist out to steal and trick and lie.

The rule here is that power comes from the ignorant people whose heads can be filled with distortions and whose actions can be controlled. By filling their heads with anti-capitalist notions, the organizer knows that these people will assume that these notions are true and then act with anger and vitriol. They can then be sent out into the streets and/or the lobbies of big businesses to fill the spaces up with angry chants and accusations. The response by the corporations would be clear:

'Get them out of the lobbies, avoid a stink in the media. We've got to appease them in some way so we can get about the business of selling things and making money.'

For the Alinsky Radical, the enemy, the capitalist manager, has got to see these people as having the power to disrupt the operation, the power to buy elsewhere, the power to do much harm by repeating lies in the media. This is where the "Have-Nots" and the community organizer can gain power.

With all these people in his lobby, the manager must find the leader of these people, try to speak with him, learn what he wants and then give it to him. When he asks for money for a local community center, he responds: 'we'd be glad to provide it, even build it for them.' When asked for jobs for the community unemployed, he responds: 'no problem, we'll find something they can do around here.'

In return, all the company wants is good publicity, articles in the paper about some of the good things the company is doing for the community, blah, blah, blah. Even better, the community organizer wants to run for office and he could sure use their support. No problem. The community business alliance has just been born and the old Marxist axiom that the capitalists will sell you the rope you intend to hang them with has been proven true.

Remember, the Alinskyites attack businesses, not because they are evil or big, but because they have economic power that the radicals want to use to finance their own goals. The Radicals do not have a right to corporate money nor do they have the moral authority to criticize any company's efforts to earn a profit. They only protest in the lobby because they know the corporation does not have a moral argument to defend itself. The Radicals pretend to be doing the "good" thing by taking upon themselves the responsibility for representing "the people". The corporation only has economic arguments that the Radicals refute with the latest bogus scientific study that "proves" the corporation is racist, xenophobic and oppressive.

Ayn Rand says:

"A disastrous intellectual package-deal, put over on us by the theoreticians of statism, is the equation of economic power with political power. You have heard it expressed in such bromides as: "A hungry man is not free," or "It makes no difference to a worker whether he takes orders from a businessman or from a bureaucrat." Most people accept these equivocations — and yet they know that the poorest laborer in America is freer and more secure than the richest commissar in Soviet Russia. What is the basic, the essential, the crucial principle that differentiates freedom from slavery? It is the principle of voluntary action versus physical coercion or compulsion."[25]

---

[25] Ayn Rand, America's Persecuted Minority: Big Business

When the left cannot distinguish between economic power and political power, they ignore the fact that economic power is not about using force against people but about using intelligence to create better products and services that improve peoples' lives. The left's model of the evil corporation portrays businesspeople as monsters who are trying to use government to gain a political advantage; ignoring the fact that if government did not have the ability to intervene into the economy, there would be no need for political power. It is the left's own policy of interfering in the economy that forces businesses and corporations to seek political power. They must, as a matter of survival, protect themselves against the oppressive tendencies of government under the leftists.

The community organizers and the government are in league with each other. Now, due to this shakedown, the corporation has just become a part of the government. It must enter into an alliance with the left in order to stay in business. So money flows to the political organizations of the left and away from investment in better products and services – in short – away from making profits.

But the attitude of the Alinsky Radicals is that they must appropriate the productive power of the corporation to themselves. They have no problem with this process because they know that their newly gained power can be a source of tremendous amounts of "cooperation". They know they can keep bashing "self-interest" and profits among "the people" while getting involved in huge transfers of "power" through the corporations who donate to their "causes". Productive power has now become political power.

The guilt-tripping, blaming, criticizing and shaming of businesses is a sinister racket. The community organizers can now make extra money by hiring out the "professional" protestors to work against competing corporations which gives them even more power. Businesses are eager to avoid problems so they eagerly make huge payments to these pesky "community organizers" who are using neighborhoods as power bases for their political careers.

The 2007-8 subprime fiasco was a case in point. It started during the '90s when community organizers floated a false study that purported to prove that banks were "red lining" poor neighborhoods filled with mostly black people. The premise of the study was that banks were only concerned with giving loans to people who were wealthy. The charge was that they cared for profit over people.

The radicals blamed the banks for racism. The banks were even accused of making these neighborhoods poor. This study was broadcast far and wide and it became an article of faith among progressive politicians that we needed to do something to help the poor.

Community organizations like ACORN, along with a number of prominent politicians had the solution. In the early '90s, a young lawyer by the name of Barack Obama went to court on behalf of ACORN and other organizations to change lending standards under an existing Act known as the Community Reinvestment Act (CRA).

The result of the lawsuit was a change in the Act that required banks to prove they were not discriminating against poor neighborhoods. Banks were given the clear message that there could be dire consequences if they did not issue more loans. Even Bill Clinton and Janet Reno got in on the action, threatening banks with Justice Department investigations if they could not prove they were issuing more loans to the poor.

ACORN then got busy expanding offices into neighborhoods all around the country to "help" the poor get home loans. This created a huge industry and ACORN did not care whether the people could pay the loans off. Their programs became re-distribution and money laundering schemes.

Another friend of Obama, one Penny Pritsker, after declaring bankruptcy in her own bank, developed the idea of packaging all of these loans for the poor into financial packages known as derivatives. This involved selling these packages to investors, getting the derivatives deemed safe investments by rating agencies (due primarily to the fact that the loans were backed by the Federal Government) through Fannie Mae and Freddie Mac (two quasi-governmental organizations led by Democratic fund raisers). Over time, the large number of these loans did stress the system.[26] [27]

Just as the community organizer who represented the poor those few years ago was running for President, someone leaked the fact that these loans were beginning to stress the system. When homeowners stopped making their payments, this exposed the fact that the derivatives were worthless and Fannie and Freddie were now insolvent. Once they collapsed, other investors decided to sell short on their stock investments and everything collapsed.

All the mortgage holders needed to do was not pay their mortgages and eventually the government would bail everyone out. And this is exactly what happened much to the shame of George W. Bush. The result of the collapse is that investors lost about ½ the value of their investments, the Republicans were blamed and a community organizer, the

[26] http://www.americanthinker.com/articles/2008/10/hedge_funds_politics_and_the_m.html
[27] http://www.americanthinker.com/articles/2008/10/what_really_happened_in_the_mo.html

individual who had orchestrated the entire fiasco, was elected President. No one even thought that he was involved in starting us on the path toward this massive collapse.

This is what I mean when I say that the Alinsky Radicals are all about power. Their power to control the media, the banks, the government and the politicians enabled them to bring the economy down setting the stage for blaming the Republicans for a policy fought for by the Alinsky Radicals in the government. Almost all media outlets put out report after report, article after article that the cause of this fiasco was the banks and Alan Greenspan who had countenanced de-regulation. There was no such de-regulation at least not enough to have caused this fiasco. What caused the fiasco was Obama and ACORN, both of whom made money by offering loans to people who otherwise would not have qualified for them.

Capitalism had failed said the Alinsky Radical in the White House and what was needed was Dodd-Frank, a set of regulations named after the two key politicians who were complicit in ensuring that the Republicans could not address the growing problems. Dodd and Frank were, in fact, two of the key culprits who had fanned the flames of the original false study and had done everything possible to bring the collapse about. All the short-sellers got rich on this scheme but not the American people. They wound up, against their will, having a massive bailout, forced down their throats.

There is a lesson in this fiasco. We should never appease a radical by agreeing that he is correct about anything. Find out where he is wrong and take a firm stand based upon the facts. Know that his goal is not to make things better but to stress the system, to play for power at any cost. If they lie about your company, correct the lie. If they picket you, picket them back.

If they come to your organization, send volunteers to their organizations. Don't use economic arguments; argue on the basis of morality and the fundamental rights of the company, the employees and the management.

Never argue that you have a fundamental obligation to make bad business decisions based upon their demands. Defend your business decisions based on sound business practices.

Refuse to grant them the power to harm your organization and do not capitulate by donating to them. If they scream that they are just trying to help the poor, argue that you help your customers more by bringing them good products and services and that is your only obligation. Defend your right to make a profit and don't give in to their demands.

You must recognize that these radical groups seek power for power's sake, not to make things better. The flesh and blood that has to pay for that power consists of corporations and their employees who are forced to deal with and appease the radicals. The false idea that your business has an obligation to accommodate the demands of these radicals is the source of their push for power.

They want you to pay for their meal ticket out of the prices you charge customers. If you did not have economic power, the power of production, they would have no desire to shake you down. Rather than donate to a radical group, use your economic power to inform the public that you have a right to exist as a profit-making company. If they violate your property rights, tell them they are on private property, ask them to leave if they are not there to conduct business, take pictures, get video, identify the individuals and press charges. Never let them off the hook by refusing to prosecute.

RULE 2: "'Never go outside the expertise of your people.' It results in confusion, fear and retreat. Feeling secure adds to the backbone of anyone. (Organizations under attack wonder why radicals don't address the "real" issues. This is why. They avoid things with which they have no knowledge.)"

My comment: Anti-rule #2. Embarrass them by forcing them outside their expertise.

The weakness of the Alinsky Radicals is that they know nothing about how to run a business, especially a large corporation. They assume that you are just a money making machine and that you have huge funds available for them to loot. They don't know about pricing, the law of supply and demand and how to create efficiencies that save money. Most importantly, they know nothing about how to create value. They know only how to shame you into giving them money. It is time to stop being shamed and fight them on your terms not theirs. You have to understand that what you are doing is moral; what they are doing is theft; immoral.

Expose the ignorance of the protestors and organizers. Ask them how much they know about the reasons for their protests and tape the answers they give. If you can ask questions of them and get answers, you can use these videos with the media to show they have no idea what it takes to run a business and that they are phonies.

The purpose of this rule is to give protesters the confidence to take a stand against you because they have no such confidence. Their only confidence is in the feigned certainty of their leaders. If the protestors were to show a false confidence in their protests, it would give the impression they know they are right. They hope this intimidates you.

But, in truth, they are mindless shills; take this opportunity to display that mindlessness by taking them out of their experience. The fact is, they are wrong, and you should use this against them.

Remember, all they want is for you to be afraid of them and for the public to be ignorant about their lies. Show that they are incapable of discussing the real issues.

More importantly, educate yourself about how to defend economic freedom and liberty. Read the chapter in this book called "Debating the Left" so you know the structure of their arguments and how to defeat them in debate.

Understand that capitalism is made possible by liberty and that everyone needs to be free in order to create a vibrant, rights-respecting society. Know this, show this and be certain why you are right. Their only certainty is in Marxism, lies, propaganda and wrong premises (See the chapter "Cultural Marxism").

My comment: Anti-rule #3. Be prepared to defend against spurious attacks based on bogus information. You'll get points if you stand on principle. You'll get points by attacking the fundamental principles of the Alinsky Radicals. Attack their use of force or moral force.

We saw a lot of this in Ferguson and Baltimore. Virtually every man on the street said the same lie. They talked about systemic and structural racism that caused the riots and crimes. This argument surprised many people because they blamed, not just white people, but the "system". This virtually silenced honest people because they had no response to these spurious charges. How can you disprove "systemic racism" when you can't even prove it? What was the solution then?

More re-distribution programs (forced expropriation). Give people political power so they can vote and change things (a false solution). Give people grant money (a false solution). Get white people out of government (a false solution). At every turn, the solution was a form of re-distribution because that is what they wanted; the power to use money to benefit themselves and their friends.

The use of spurious accusations is part of their strategy. These charges are intended to freeze their opposition which enables them to take charge of the conversation. Remember, their singular goal in the protest is to make you capitulate; to make America capitulate to their demands. They know that protest breeds government spending and they want that money.

Who benefits from re-distributed dollars from taxpayers and corporations? Groups of Marxist radicals who will only give us more of the same. Giving money to these radicals will create more riots, more grants, more programs and more re-distribution. You don't think they'll stop demanding more money do you?

These groups are turning American communities into battlefields. They are doing it intentionally and carving out territory for themselves; territory that they will rule with an iron hand, without government, without police, without law and without order.

Do you think that an intelligent businessperson will want to put a business or factory there knowing that doing so will make him a target? Do you wonder why businesses fly from the inner cities? Look at Detroit neighborhoods and see what happens when radicals get control of government.

RULE 4: "'Make the enemy live up to its own book of rules.'

If the rule is that every letter gets a reply, send 30,000 letters. You can kill them with this because no one can possibly obey all of their own rules. (This is a serious rule. The besieged entity's very credibility and reputation is at stake, because if activists catch it lying or not living up to its commitments, they can continue to chip away at the damage.)"

My comment: Anti-rule #4. Never apologize for making a profit and put out a position statement that you can repeat whenever necessary. The only way to fight this is to assert the value and importance of making a profit and insist that you and your stockholders believe in keeping those profits without having them extorted under threat of protest.

The biggest mistake you can make is to agree with their basic premise. In this context, their basic premise is collectivism. They think you owe it to the collective to sacrifice your profits for them. If you think you can compromise with them on these issues, you can't. To agree with their collectivism is to make yourself into a profit-making hypocrite. Indeed, the rule book they are talking about is not your rule book but theirs. It is the rulebook that says making a profit is a crime. This is why it is important to stand up for your right to profits and defend it as moral and proper. Then, they can't use the rule book against you.

The purpose of this rule is to create contradictions that put the American businessperson in a no-win situation. They want to keep presenting you with contradictions in your actions that violate that "rule" that you are your brother's keeper. They want to shame you for things you do out of self-interest.

This puts you in a bad situation. You don't run a business for the sake of helping your brother. You don't work to help your brother. You do these things out of self-interest and if they can continually accuse you of being selfish, then they have you. You are their slave. This is why you should never apologize for your self-interest. You should stand up for the principle that your freedom, your self-interest, is your justification for improving the lives of your customers.

Understand their principle: they want to make charges against you that can't be proven and that have no response. They know that accusing you of not caring for "your brother" will keep you off balance. It is a charge that can be repeated over and over to great effect. You must be ready for it.

Businesspeople must stop being cowards about making profits. They seem to always give in and proclaim that indeed they *are* their brother's keeper. Then they give the radicals hundreds of thousands of dollars in money for "programs" to help the poor. What they don't realize is that it isn't about helping people; it is about shaming you into giving power to them. That power is the noose upon which you hang yourself every time.

As Ayn Rand says:

"As a group, businessmen have been withdrawing for decades from the ideological battlefield, disarmed by the deadly combination of altruism and Pragmatism. Their public policy has consisted in appeasing, compromising and apologizing: appeasing their crudest, loudest antagonists; compromising with any attack, any lie, any insult; apologizing for their own existence. Abandoning the field of ideas to their enemies, they have been relying on lobbying, i.e., on private manipulations, on pull, on seeking momentary favors from government officials. Today, the last group one can expect to fight for capitalism is the capitalists."[28]

---

[28] Ayn Rand, The Ayn Rand Letter, The Moratorium on Brains

So how do you keep them from winning? You start by defending your right to your property and especially your right to make a living and to keep your earnings.

Again, we are back to individual rights. You start by not feeling guilty for making a living, and especially, by not feeling guilty for being successful in business and in life. Once you see that you have rights and those rights involve your living for yourself first, you can resist their attempts to ridicule and shame you (See chapter "Altruism").

RULE 5: "'Ridicule is man's most potent weapon.' There is no defense. It's irrational. It's infuriating. It also works as a key pressure point to force the enemy into concessions. (Pretty crude, rude and mean, huh? They want to create anger and fear.)"

My comment: Anti-rule #5. If they ridicule you, point out that ridicule is not an argument and insist that they provide a clear statement that explains their goals. If they continue to ridicule you, expose that ridicule as being illogical and unclear.

Ad hominem attacks are not valid forms of argument and they violate clear thinking. Ridicule is what charlatans do. It is the barbarian's way of "winning" an argument. That the Alinsky Radicals accept this rule only reveals the utter intellectual bankruptcy of this radical movement. They can be defeated by a large dose of what they have no argument against: logic and reason.

Alinsky's premise here is that ridicule is proper against someone who is utterly evil and dictatorial. Educators have spent decades building up this false charge against corporations. They have done it by means of a constant barrage of criticism that charges capitalism with hypocrisy and nefarious dealings; most of which are false. You should assert your honesty and refuse to enable their real hypocrisy.

The reason they ridicule you is because they want you to consider yourself evil. They want you to fear their false opinion. You should be certain about how moral you are. Fight their ridicule by being an honest person.

RULE 6: "'A good tactic is one your people enjoy.' They'll keep doing it without urging and come back to do more. They're doing their thing, and will even suggest better ones. (Radical activists, in this sense, are no different than any other human being. We all avoid "un-fun" activities, and but we revel at and enjoy the ones that work and bring results.)"

My comment: Anti-radical Rule #6. Tell the truth and you will make the radical feel rightfully ashamed for his tactics of deception. Shame him with the ridicule he deserves for trying to pry money out of your company or the taxpayers.

The goal here for the organizer is to ensure that people continue to protest. They have to make it fun, perhaps feed the protesters, take them to a park, have a party, etc. This rule can be easily mitigated by a simple explanation to these people that they are really not accomplishing their goals of helping anyone and are in fact hurting the very people they claim to represent.

Re-distribution is evil and we need to keep making that case. A person cannot take pleasure in destruction if he knows he is gaining the ire of honest people. Deliver that ire to them in spades. Make sure they don't enjoy confronting you.

This tactic essentially says they know there is no content to their arguments except worn out saws against capitalism and the profit motive. It says they are not able to justify the protest except to say they are "fighting against corporate greed". Take the position that there is no such thing as corporate greed. Reduce their argument to the "nothing" that it is.

This tactic has worked well for them in the streets of Ferguson and Baltimore. A plethora of groups arose out of those protests, each having their own t-shirts and baseball caps and each proclaiming they were working for "the people" or "the neighborhood" but with a Marxist flavoring and ethic. They talked about solidarity and struggle without being specific about what it was they were struggling against. One thing is clear, each of these new groups will soon be applying for a government grant from the Administration or a leftist foundation.

Another tactic you can try is to do whatever you can to make it uncomfortable for them to protest you. Change the physical environment, if you can, to place obstacles in their ways or get them outside into the rain. Close the business temporarily and shut off the air conditioning or heat. If they are violating property rights, call the police, have them arrested and prosecute. Make sure it is as uncomfortable and unpleasant as possible for them.

RULE 7: "'A tactic that drags on too long becomes a drag.' Don't become old news. (Even radical activists get bored. So to keep them excited and involved, organizers are constantly coming up with new tactics.)"

My comment: Anti-rule #7. Radical tactics can be easily defeated by a strong philosophical argument that refutes the basis of the tactic. Again, they need to keep their tactics fresh because they want to keep those they protest against off-guard; and they need to keep their protestors from getting bored. It is indeed, boring and a waste of time to be standing in the streets looking angry and playing for a camera. Eventually, they will learn that they are doing it for nothing except the glorification of some street organizer or community charlatan.

Show your resolve by posting a "position paper" defending your company on individual rights positions. Publish your opinion in newspapers, take out adds defending your rights, do everything you can to outlast them and/or kill the protest by defeating it intellectually.

Eventually, these people will have to get back to figuring out how to get a meal. They will soon tire and go home despondent. Wait them out. Be there when the "goodies" run out and they have to leave.

RULE 8: "'Keep the pressure on. Never let up.' Keep trying new things to keep the opposition off balance. As the opposition masters one approach, hit them from the flank with something new. (Attack, attack, attack from all sides, never giving the reeling organization a chance to rest, regroup, recover and re-strategize.)"

My comment: Anti-rule #8. Keep the intellectual pressure on the radicals. Prepare in advance a contingency program for what you will do should your company ever become a target of these radicals. Use the suggestions in this book and be ready to move into action as soon as there is any indication that they are coming. Never let up and never capitulate. Never grant them a single Marxist premise.

Disagree with and fight their coercive tactics. Train some of your people on how to argue with the radicals on the streets and keep these people there browbeating them relentlessly until they get tired of arguing with you. Make sure your arguments are strong.

This rule for radicals assumes that you are wrong and they are right. Do not allow them to get away with this view. Insist that you are right and that you refuse to be coerced. The Radicals are only about setting the foundation for forcing you to give money to them. They are only about extortion. Never grant a semblance of credit to them for thinking they are doing good. Make them feel guilty for associating with radicals and violent extremists. In yourself, let them see an intellectual extremist who knows that he is right in fighting against their coercion. Insist they are doing wrong to your company and this country. Give them no quarter that they can use to further attack you. Make them feel guilty as hell – because they are guilty.

Get the names of the local leadership of the radicals and have your lawyer write them a letter threatening a personal law suit against him or her. Tell them the consequences of their actions for them personally and in their own lives. Refer to actual laws that they are violating. Press charges when possible and go for the jugular – their personal funds.

The best way to disagree with the Alinsky Radicals is to make a statement of principles to support your economic activities. Ensure that these principles are based on liberty and fight for the right to exist as a businessman, an employee or as a private citizen. Find ways to express your statement of principles through advertising, pamphleteering, speeches and other public appearances and stand your ground.

The thing about a bully is that he is a weakling. As soon as you show resolve, he melts into a coward who is afraid of life. As long as he is able to get the moral high ground by using altruism against you, he will pretend to be a moral authority. Once you refuse to grant him that power, he has nothing to say.

Rand:

"We cannot fight against collectivism, unless we fight against its moral base: altruism. We cannot fight against altruism, unless we fight against its epistemological base: irrationalism. We cannot fight against anything, unless we fight for something—and what we must fight for is the supremacy of reason, and a view of man as a rational being. These are philosophical issues. The philosophy we need is a conceptual equivalent of America's sense of life. To propagate it, would require the hardest intellectual battle. But isn't that a magnificent goal to fight for?"[29]

RULE 9: "'The threat is usually more terrifying than the thing itself.' Imagination and ego can dream up many more consequences than any activist. (Perception is reality. Large organizations always prepare a worst-case scenario, something that may be furthest from the activists' minds. The upshot is that the organization will expend enormous time and energy, creating in its own collective mind the direst of conclusions. The possibilities can easily poison the mind and result in demoralization.)"

My comment: Anti-rule #9. Remember you are not guilty of anything and you must fight for the moral high ground. The worst premise of Rule 9 is "perception is reality".

The idea that perception is reality is an old and untrue pragmatist premise. Perception is either correct or it is flawed. If it is flawed, it must be corrected so the individual can take

---

[29] Ayn Rand, The Ayn Rand Letter, Don't Let it Go

appropriate action. One cannot accept a "perception" that is a misidentification of reality. If the perception is that your company is evil, that statement is either true or false. If it is false, then don't accept it and do whatever you can to fight it. If you don't fight it, then you will lose against charlatans who want to take advantage of your inability to fight for the real percept.

The idea that one must accept the perception of a Marxist is also wrong. This approach is a way for them to gain the moral upper hand by confronting you with a moral argument that you are not supposed to challenge. Challenge it. Force them to prove it. Yelling and screaming and chanting don't prove anything.

As a businessman, or as an employee, you are the moral agent who has taken an idea and made it work. You offer services and products that people need and you have earned the business of your customers. Your best argument is your competence. Their best argument is that you are not sure of yourself against their assertion of moral authority. Do not be morally intimidated; be morally certain. Know the correct percept and fight for it.

The radicals are trying to muscle in on your hard work. They want to skim off the profits and use it for their goals. Never allow them an opportunity to declare moral equivalency with you. They are immoral and you should treat them that way. You are morally superior because you work hard, honestly and productively. They want to steal from you the value you have created. This makes them morally inferior to you.

They want you to think that "perception is reality". When you accept this notion, then the only thing you can do is capitulate to their deliberate effort to create an incorrect perception over something your company does. You have the power to correct someone who is creating a bad perception.

RULE 10: "'If you push a negative hard enough, it will push through and become a positive.' Violence from the other side can win the public to your side because the public sympathizes with the underdog. (Unions used this tactic.

Peaceful [albeit loud] demonstrations during the heyday of unions in the early to mid-20th Century incurred management's wrath, often in the form of violence that eventually brought public sympathy to their side.)"

My comment: Anti-Rule #10. Never respond in kind to a provocation. This is another pragmatist notion that if you repeat a lie often enough it becomes reality and then you have to respond to that reality and that is beneficial to them. Again, not only is perception not necessarily reality but the Big Lie is still a lie.

The question to ask is "what is a negative in this context?" A negative is a divisive issue that they have concocted out of thin air. They must manufacture these negatives because there are no divisive negatives in a free society. There is no systemic exploitation, discrimination or exclusions. In a truly free society, people are free to make their own decisions and then suffer or benefit from the consequences. They do not blame another "class" for their problems because life is a process of growth and improvement, not one of conflict with others. It is not a zero-sum society.

To accomplish division, the radicals "assume" that some sort of exploitation and deceit is being imposed on people. So when they "push" a negative hard, they are pushing a lie. The only way this can work is if you, the target, let it. Neither history nor sound economics validate the left's lies and the only way to stop them from pushing these false narratives is to learn history and understand economic principles so that you can correct the lies.

The riots in Baltimore are a good example of this. As soon as the triggering event became known nationally, a plethora of groups swarmed into Baltimore in order to participate in the riots. These groups used this opportunity to loot and destroy in order to send a message of fake outrage over a situation that had hardly been resolved at that point. The goal was to invent the perception of an epidemic of violence by police against blacks. They wanted to "push" the lie in order to bring about government spending from which these groups could benefit. The alliance between Alinsky radicals, criminals and gangs, not to mention local politicians was evident. Few Americans were fooled by this display; nor were they convinced by all the rhetoric about systemic violence and structural racism. This was all about "pushing the negatives hard".

Remember, the Alinsky Radicals are always trying to provoke a response in order to gin up public support. They have no problem using vitriol, feigned moral outrage, violence and the threat of violence to push the negatives hard. The media will help them. This tactic is vicious and they have no moral compunction against creating incidents that they can exploit. Never react emotionally but when the law is violated obtain the help of law enforcement and prosecute. For them, prosecution means having to defend themselves in court and being labeled a criminal. The more Americans fight back legally against them, the better; the more Americans take the initiative against them, the fewer people will they enlist as protestors. Who wants to go to jail?

RULE 11: "'The price of a successful attack is a constructive alternative.' Never let the enemy score points because you're caught without a solution to the problem. (Old saw: If you're not part of the solution, you're part of the problem. Activist organizations have an agenda, and their strategy is to hold a place at the table, to be given a forum to wield their power. So, they have to have a compromise solution.)"

My comment: Anti-radical Rule #11. Be an Elliott Ness for individual rights. Never compromise with gangster tactics. Do not give them a seat at the table. Don't invite them to your meetings, don't pay protection money and do use the law to fight them at every opportunity. In your contingency planning, you should also have a solution ready for whatever "solution" they offer. Never negotiate but make your "solution" known publicly through press releases. The solution to their violence is that they go to jail or cease and desist. The solution to their protests is for them to go home. The solution to their demands is to not even think about giving in.

Keep in mind, that the Alinsky Radicals do not have solutions. They only have money laundering schemes and re-distribution of your profits to them. And it is always your money that they will use to wield their power. Once you bring them to the table, you are only going to get anti-solutions, power schemes that benefit them and work toward your detriment. If they claim that they will not relent, then tell them that the only "solution" to this standoff is for your company to move to a friendlier business environment.

If you are being extorted, say so openly and fight in the name of your rights firstly and in the name of civilized behavior secondly. Finally, fight in the name of the people they claim to be helping and point out that they are not helping them but enslaving them. Also, fight in the name of the neighborhood that is being corrupted by gangster tactics, and speak out about the harm they do when scaring businesses away. Who wants to do business in a neighborhood dominated by criminal gangs and Marxist agitators?

RULE 12: "'Pick the target, freeze it, personalize it, and polarize it.' Cut off the support network and isolate the target from sympathy. Go after people and not institutions; people hurt faster than institutions. (This is cruel, but very effective. Direct, personalized criticism and ridicule works.)"

My comment: Anti-radical Rule #12. Let their tactics of polarization work against them by pointing them out. Be ready to defend yourself against unearned attacks that seek to paint you into a moral corner. You can also pick a target, freeze it, personalize it, and polarize it. You can stand for civility and reason while they stand for shakedown and extortion. Don't be afraid to polarize them for what they are doing. Find out who the leaders are and make it personal. Write articles against their nefarious activities. Exposing them is not making martyrs of them.

They need to make you into the evil enemy so they can obtain the moral high ground. But let's examine the four maxims more closely:

Pick the target

The Alinsky radicals will pick targets that are vulnerable by the standard of altruism; that means targets that can be criticized for pursuing profits ahead of people. These include banks that can be shaken down for cash, large franchise-based corporations like McDonald's and companies providing products to consumers. The radicals will pick a variety of charges that they can make against these corporations and then stoke those charges into "legitimacy" using the leftist media. Once the target is picked, constant picketing and protests can be launched, lawyers can bring lawsuits and newspapers will write stories to "validate" the charges.

Freeze it

The concept of freezing the target means that the radicals want to impose so much guilt against the corporation that the general public begins to think the organization is an evil player worthy of boycott, law suits and punitive legislation. The point is to make the company completely inert and unable to defend itself in the court of public opinion so that it has no option but to capitulate to the radicals.

Again, it must be noted that the charges made by the radicals are fundamentally false. They are charges that have been stoked up and brought to such a fever pitch that the company has lost the ability to defend itself and can only "settle out of court". This is called being morally frozen, unable to act and unable to defend yourself.

Personalize it

Again, the idea of choosing a target is intended to focus on a specific individual who could be identified as the person responsible for the "evil" supposedly being done by a capitalist organization. By focusing on an individual, picketing his or her home, the shaming is brought to a new lower level. This puts the onus on the decisions of one individual with power and seeks to divest this individual of power and coerce him or her to act in the way the radicals want.

Polarize it

Polarizing the target means putting them on the losing side of the class struggle. This tactic can be understood if we look at the treatment by the radicals of Republicans. At every turn, Republican opposition has been polarized. The administration is seeking a spending program to "help the poor" and make money available for programs run by the radicals. Republican opposition to this might be principled, correct and moral but the radicals will polarize the issues; they will claim that the Republicans hate the poor; that they are trying to throw grandma off a cliff; put people out on the street; cause babies to starve because they are against a program that will help them. The Radicals conveniently ignore the fact that the Obama program is a boondoggle designed to provide grant money to radical organizations. They ignore the fact that very little of the money will actually reach the poor. They ignore the fact that the money being spent belongs to the taxpayer and the program would remove investment dollars from the economy doing long-term damage that hurts the poor even more.

How does one answer this? How can we work toward a society of freedom and capitalism when the enemies of freedom argue in the name of freedom? They claim to represent the poor, the descendants of slaves, tribal members and the disenfranchised. Yet, their solutions for these people involve force against others. They follow the altruist maxim that men should sacrifice for others, and if they don't, they should be punished and ridiculed in some way for their selfish ways.

To defeat altruism, we must defeat the Alinsky Radicals. They will never change their minds. They will always fight for the eventual tyranny. A more concerted effort must be made to practice defeat these treacherous tactics with reasoned arguments that refute the Radical's policies.

This effort has to come from the grass roots, from an educated citizenry eager for freedom. We know that the leftists are corrupt. We know they are deceivers. We know they lie, and we know that some of them are gangsters and crooks. This leaves them open to exposure. You can pick a target, freeze it, personalize it and polarize it. It may take new media, an ambitious reporter, a think tank, a new Tea Party organization, a private investigator and a journalist hungry for truth; and the truth is out there to be dug out.

This last rule represents the tactic of Marxists, union organizers and fascists. They all claim to be the true defenders of the people. Which brings us to the more important question: How can the left be disenfranchised long-term? The only way is for us to lift the mask of their pretensions and expose them for the gangsters and crooks their leaders are. It isn't enough to fight them in the streets. They are like chameleons; you can defeat them in one cause or one tactic, but they'll be back protesting something else tomorrow because people give them the platforms from which to speak. We need to expose their sabotage and lies so people will realize they aren't adding anything good to the discussion.

The true problems in society today are people like the Alinsky Radicals and their war against individual rights, contract law and property ownership. The damage done to the economy by the constant drain of investment capital toward false goals is also a real problem. The creation of poverty by government spending is a real problem; the aggrandizement of liars and cheats is a real problem. These can only be fought by adherence to the principles of liberty and by the reestablishment of individual rights.

You should certainly take the moral high ground away from the radicals by exposing their immoral tactics and hypocrisy. Do not let them turn every invented emergency into a re-distribution of guilt. You must defend your legal and moral rights. You cannot allow them to take the moral high ground.

The Alinksy Radicals are not about making communities better; they are about gaining control of businesses and communities and forcing them to pay money. They are the children of union organizers and criminals. They are gangsters operating under cover of charitable organizations looking to extort money from you; they are money launderers and crooks. If you capitulate to them, your business or community cannot thrive.

Some of these people will stop at nothing to get their way. Some are fully capable of violence and murder. Your best answer to them, in addition to staunch resistance is to educate yourself about proper government and proper community relations. Fight against the idea that you have an obligation to accept a gang bent on extortion in your community. Learn to defend your rights by reading the history of our nation, understand the principles of free trade, the pursuit of happiness and civilized behavior and recognize that we must either have a society that defends individual rights or we have no society at all. You may have to become a philosopher to defend yourself, but these radicals count on your not knowing how to fight for your rights. They need for you to be weak and guilty so they can control you.

The true long-term solution to Alinsky-style radicalism is education of our children. We must ensure that future generations are able to think, to reason, to apply logic and to engage in real science (not pseudo-science). This takes a repudiation of mysticism and the refusal to fall under the spell of another group of radicals, the religious right.

The separation of church and state created a "secular" society and we are still largely secular in nature. The answer to the leftist radicals is not a return to religious values, the imposition of the Ten Commandments, the public support of private charities, but the reinstitution of individual rights. Only individuals, firm in the conviction that individual rights are paramount will be able to resist the advance of shakedown artists and potential dictators.

A civilized society is characterized by a focus on the individual and what he can do for his own survival. This requires that he gain knowledge, get a good education and be free to act. When knowledge is combined with self-interest; that is when we get real morality. That is when the individual is autonomous and begins earning his future by offering real value in exchange for real value. Only a free society unencumbered by those who want to re-distribute "just a little bit of your money", can be a moral society.

I have pointed out before that our society is decidedly not in a moral crisis. Overall, it is a free society struggling to respect that freedom. Even today, the only moral crisis we have is the crisis of people trying to shackle us with high taxes and re-distribution. A totally free society (meaning a limited government) leaves people free to decide about moral actions for themselves.

This is morality in action and, even today, our morality is evident by the fact that many of us have jobs; that we have to be good at our jobs; that we have to find products and services that improve our lives and that, overwhelmingly, we routinely make viable decisions about what is right for our lives. A free society will be a moral society and as people experience that freedom day-in-and-day-out, they will increasingly make more correct decisions, create better products and enjoy their lives and comfort.

If we truly want a moral society then we will let people be free to make their own decisions. We will recognize the truth that if someone makes a decision harmful to himself, he will eventually learn from his mistakes and correct them. That's part of what freedom means. I may not like what you do but whatever decision you make, you will suffer the consequences or enjoy the benefits. That's what being free is about. The Alinsky Radicals and their street crowds need to learn that lesson too.

In his Own Words

"I regard the welfare state as an abomination, as morally evil. I do not base morality on the Sermon of the Mount, and I do not put forth a moral case in terms of the lame, the halt and the blind…you have to first say "what does the healthy, unafflicted individual require?" You cannot shackle those who are able to function, allegedly in the name of helping the weak, because then you will wipe out the whole human race. If compassion for those who cannot survive on their own is your value, the first thing you should do is take the shackles off of the people who are able to think, and produce and create the wealth that everyone requires to survive including the weak." — Dr. Leonard Peikoff, Debate 1984, Socialism vs. Capitalism

The above quote should put the philosophy of the Alinsky Radicals into context. To get further clarification on how evil that philosophy is, we should look at the ideas of one of their most illustrious leaders. His name is Barack Obama.

"Focusing your life solely on making a buck shows a certain poverty of ambition. It asks too little of yourself. Because it's only when you hitch your wagon to something larger than yourself that you realize your true potential."

This quote has all the elements common in altruistic statements, not the least of which is that it sounds naïve and even ludicrous. First, you'll notice the criticism of selfishness, using the straw man of "making a buck". This is intended to minimize the value of self-sufficiency by calling it, in essence, cheap and valueless. The idea is that there is something morally inferior in "making a buck" and that, by contrast, serving others is of the highest moral value. This is intended to make you feel guilty for living. Then by stating that such an attitude reflects a "poverty of ambition", he advances the guilt to the "sin" of personal ambition. It is statements like this that cause the ruin of nations. Such statements are without merit and logical consistency. They are proof of the low moral status and intellectual dishonesty of the man who would declare himself superior to the man who earns his own way.

This blanket judgment reflects disrespect for the individual and an attitude that making "mere money" is immoral. Better to give it to the critic to do "real" good with it. Such an attitude expressed by a President of the USA indicates that it is a common attitude, essentially, a common prejudice. That someone of his "stature" can make such an expression openly and without fear of dissent says much about the hatred of the individual in our society and the dominance of altruism as a moral philosophy. One is supposed to conclude without reason that "it is not about you" when it comes to moral living. It is only about others. Proof? No proof is needed from the person who has ascended the pedestal of moral posturing.

There is absolutely nothing wrong with being ambitious about one's life. In fact, having ambition to do better in life is a highly moral sentiment. *And, it should be said, with emphasis that, if wanting to "make a buck" is a bad thing, then I side with "making a buck". In fact, if anyone wants to make money, he will quickly discover that, in order to do so, he must create values and trade them honestly.* Using the "selfishness is evil" strawman, as the President does, is the essence of demagoguery and arrogance.

What the President seeks to accomplish through this statement is to elevate self-sacrifice to a level of respect higher than the act of being successful through trade. It exposes a dearth of understanding of what it means to actually do good things. It also exposes the certainty that he, the President, intends to collect the sacrifices.

"We can't drive our SUVs and eat as much as we want and keep our homes on 72 degrees at all times... and then just expect that other countries are going to say OK. That's not leadership. That's not going to happen."

My first question is why not? Who is to decide what we "should" do? Here you see the collectivism that the President holds as a fundamental premise. The idea that we owe it to "the planet" or "the world" to tailor our actions, even our enjoyments, to *their* moral judgments is more than ludicrous – it is a downright insult. Yet, the President takes it as given that Americans should not be self-sufficient and self-directed; instead we should care first what the world thinks about our use of resources. Even worse, according to him, our use of resources is a moral black spot upon us; it is theft and the world is perfectly justified in having an opinion about it. Ours sounds like a very arrogant planet when it tells us what to do with our earnings and how to enjoy our lives. Frankly, Barack, I don't give a damn what you or the planet thinks.

Indeed, according to the President, we should engage in "true leadership" on this issue and voluntarily lower our standard of living so we can leave something for those who will also be denigrated for using energy in the future. In fact, this argument holds (through foreign aid and other programs) that we should pay the rest of the world by providing them with the infrastructure that would enable them to catch up with us in our use of energy. In other words, we should lower our expectations, stop our progress and voluntarily lower our standard of living while also spending our savings to bring the rest of the world into the 17th Century.

Americans are no more evil than any other human beings on the planet. History has shown that Americans are among some of the most open, most rational, most intelligent and successful creatures on the planet. Their advances and production have already lifted other people up and made their lives easier. We have sold the world millions of products that improve their lives, save them time and lighten their loads. We have even shown them an example of what happiness is and how to achieve it. Not only this, we are the cleanest, most energy-efficient and productive people on the planet. Far from taking from others, Americans give much more *to* others than any other people – much more than many of those "others" deserve; and we do it while pursuing our self-interest and improving our own lives

The President has an essentially third-world mindset, a cold war, almost pro-Soviet mindset convinced by pro-Soviet cold war propaganda points, most of which were uttered during the 50s, 60s and 70s (while the Soviet Union was propagandizing against the USA to forcibly expand its empire). Most such propaganda was deliberately anti-American and anti-imperialist, without proof or historical veracity, full of altruism and the demand that America sacrifice itself to the world. These statements were all lies that reflect not just anti-Americanism, but anti-capitalism, anti-egoism and anti-success. They portray capitalism as militaristic and needing to conquer territory when, in fact, capitalism routinely earns new customers by offering them better products.

"I think when you spread the wealth around, it's good for everybody."

This statement assumes that wealth belongs to society. It dismisses the value of the individual even while encouraging people to work hard. It also makes a false promise; that wealth re-distribution is good for everyone.

Wealth re-distribution is not good for the producer of that wealth. It keeps him from using his money wisely to generate additional economic benefit and, instead, gives the money to someone who will not spend it wisely. It assumes there is economic benefit from spending rather than from investing. And since there is no such thing as the "common good" re-distribution does not benefit society "as a whole".

With the vast preponderance of dictatorships and mixed economies today, it is not the fault of productive people that some others are poor. So, this argument about a disparity of wealth is essentially corrupt and false. This disparity has more to do with the preponderance of societies built on force, plunder and exploitation of their own people. It has more to do with re-distribution than with the lack of it. We do not need more sacrifice.

Through his call for re-distribution, the President expresses the economic philosophy of John Maynard Keynes who held that economies can be manipulated and managed by government through tax expropriation, regulation and monetary policy. It holds that government technocrats know how to make an economy work efficiently while individuals only think of themselves.

Keynesian principles, at their base, violate Says Law which states that production creates markets not consumption. Says Law is an expression of the economic principle that production must come before consumption and that money and markets should be left in the hands of producers rather than re-distributed to the consumer in an effort to "stimulate" the economy.

The re-distribution of money by the government is the cause of many problems for the economy. Not only is it an expression of the concept of altruism, the idea that some must sacrifice for others, but it reduces the amount of money available for productive economic decisions and creates the very poverty the government claims to be addressing.

"If you were successful, somebody along the line gave you some help... Somebody helped to create this unbelievable American system that we have that allowed you to thrive. Somebody invested in roads and bridges. If you've got a business - you didn't build that. Somebody else made that happen."

This is one of the most commented upon statements ever made by the President. Its purpose is to diminish individual achievement and elevate collective action as the solution to survival for man. It is a clear indication of his Marxist philosophy and of the influence on him of Rousseau (the social contract). The argument implies that the individual could never accomplish his specific goals in life without the help of society and because so he should dedicate his life to serving society in thanks for what it has given him.

The truth is that the conclusion does not follow. Despite the fact that we live in a society built by those who came before us, we are still responsible for the actions we take. Those people who came before did not build our philosophical and social infrastructure merely for our sake as a gift. These so-called gifts came to us as a result of the initiative and desire of past citizens who wanted to succeed in their own lives. None of this diminishes the stark fact that each of us must take the initiative to succeed in life and to the extent that we do succeed, each of us is responsible for that success even if we have benefitted from the actions of others.

Every man is capable of accomplishing his goals in life and many do it through education, hard work and individual achievement – not through the assistance of society. In fact, many people succeed despite society rather than because of it. There are many examples of this including Steve Jobs, whose company created much of the new technologies that are revolutionizing American life today.

The government could never have created such marvels as the automobile, railroads, steam engines, electrical grids, petroleum products all of which create the infrastructure that many of us count on to live better lives. Yet, even in our time, each person is responsible for using his mind and to whatever extent he or she does so, the individual is fully responsible for the results of those actions. He owes nothing to society that he has not paid for through his productive ability. Man is not a product of a collective mind. He is a product of the thinking he does during his own lifetime. It does not take a village; it takes freedom.

"But on a more basic level, every American can do something even simpler. As we go about our daily lives, we must remember that our countrymen are still serving, still fighting, still putting their lives on the line for all of us. ...Let us never forget to always remember and to be worthy of the sacrifice they make in our name."

As a Korean War Veteran, I take issue with this form of expression. For instance, I didn't consider my time in the military to be putting my life on the line for other Americans. I considered my service to be, first, for my rights and for my family's rights and for those I loved and only then for all Americans. But, more basically, I was putting my life on the line for the freedom that I wanted to experience as an individual. I was fighting for freedom, not sacrificing for others. I was a paid professional offering a service, protection to my fellow citizens, not as a sacrifice but as a professional service that I was trained to provide. Had I not been paid for my service, I would have been a slave.

I've often asked myself, what does it mean to be worthy of the "sacrifice they make in our name"? I don't ask my fellow Americans to be "worthy" of any sacrifice. I am successful as a soldier when the people I protect live great lives in freedom. I am successful when they are free to enjoy their lives. I don't ask them to sacrifice in return for my giving them freedom.

They don't have to do anything to be worthy of the freedom my actions made possible. Freedom is not a gift born in sacrifice but a right of every man. They are already free people by nature of the fact that they are human beings. I don't elevate sacrifice to the position of a high value when I work to keep them free. Why does the President?

The answer to this, in my opinion, is that the President values sacrifice but not freedom. His ideological foundation is essentially a worship of the negative. He worships more the people who receive the benefits of sacrifice rather than those who earn those benefits through their own work. Like many radical progressives, the President has learned to use sacrifice as a virtue. He believes in sacrifice and wants to ensure that the American people transition from selfishness to self-sacrifice as he transforms America into a society based, not on freedom, but on re-distribution.

Certainly, every soldier who dies in defense of America has his own reasons for being in the military. Whatever the reason, it should be respected in the sense that no one should diminish the value and import of a career dedicated to the defense of the nation. Our nation is unique in the annals of nations because it is virtually the only "free nation" made up of autonomous individuals and this makes it worth defending. Any person who decides on a career in the military should do so freely and according to his own inclinations. No one has a right to assert that each and every one of these individuals is engaged in a willful act of self-sacrifice. The President is trying, through his statements, to expropriate the work and energy of everyone who fought and died in combat and to use that work and energy to advance the opposite of freedom. To interpret these lives as sacrifices is to misinterpret them and use them for one's own political purposes. To ask people to see only sacrifice as a value is to dishonor the men who died to maintain the pursuit of happiness. Our soldiers fight for freedom; they fight for an un-sacrificial society; the first such society in the history of the world.[30]

The efforts by radical progressives to transform society from one of freedom to one of collectivism will put the nation on a track toward failure. This is because the basic principle of the nanny state, from each according to his ability to each according to his needs, creates failure and economic depression all around. Once this failure hits a society, the only thing left is the rule of the gun

---

[30] Read my book, Defending American Values for a fuller statement of the proper attitude for military and first responders to "serving" in the military. https://amzn.to/2ymHywf

Contradictions and Blinders

Since the advent of capitalism there have always been naysayers. The church, for instance, even before capitalism, looked askance at the concept of usury (loaning money at interest) and sought to outlaw the practice. For the Church, usury was considered immoral.

This attitude on the part of the church must have been one of the reasons why the Dark Ages were "dark". Consider also, the impact on living standards, innovation, new and better products, and you can see that restricting the practice of lending money can be a very harmful policy. Likewise, merchants who bought products for resale were also considered to be shysters, cheats and thieves. It is interesting to note that these restrictions on commerce during Christendom were made in the name of morality.

This view certainly had a negative influence on the lives of Jews. Because the Church viewed them as the killers of Jesus, Jews were often forbidden to engage in legal commerce. This created a black market that had to be hidden from the prying eyes of the Church. This is also why Jews were unfairly tarnished as corrupt, thieving, cheating types of people. It wasn't that they were crooks; they simply had no other way to earn a living. It is also telling that "what it took to survive" was an illegal form of capitalism.

If restrictions on trade can harm Jews like it did, how can we advocate similar restrictions against all men who seek to earn a profit today; and how can we look away from the damage done to those who must pay for the right to live?

When Marx came onto the scene around the middle of the 19th century, he picked up a lot of the dominant ideas in the culture (about trade) in order to create his eclectic mish mash known as revolutionary Marxism. We will again recall the Mises quote:

"Since Science and Logic had argued against Socialism, it was imperative to devise a system which could be relied on to defend it against such unpalatable criticism. This was the task which Marxism undertook to perform. It had three lines of procedure. First, it denied that Logic is universally valid for all mankind and for all ages. Thought, it stated, was determined by the class interests. The type of reasoning which had refuted the socialist idea was "revealed" as "bourgeois" reasoning, an apology for Capitalism. Secondly, it laid it down that the dialectical development led of necessity to Socialism, that the aim and end of all history was the socialization of the means of production by the expropriation of the expropriators – the negation of negation. Finally, it was ruled that no one should be allowed to put forward, as the Utopians had done, any definite proposals for the construction of the Socialist Promised Land. Since the coming of Socialism was inevitable, Science would best renounce all attempt to determine its nature"[31]

Marxist anti-capitalism is fraught with anti-mind prejudice. A good case can be made that the medieval attitudes against profit, usury and merchandising were carried straight into Marxism. Yet, as Mises tells us, Marx needed more. To "prove" his morality, he needed the sanction of both history and science, and he sought to construct a political and economic philosophy that could not be refuted. Only reality has refuted it.

For the present, we should understand that Marx is the

---

[31] Socialism by Ludwig von Mises, Liberty Classics Hardcover, Page 6

inspiration behind the far left that has recently captured the Democratic Party and the nation. This conquest was not easily won, especially considering communism's defeat at the hands of Reagan during the '80s. The '60s radicals who educated today's leading leftists were successful in taking over the universities. Using Marx's three essential premises as identified by Mises, today's university professors are nothing more than modern versions of the medieval Catholic Bishops who outlawed commerce because they thought it was the realm of the devil. Today, the Alinsky bishops clandestinely offer "socialism" and fascism, both of which bring the modern version of the medieval economic abyss. Under the mantle of an inevitable victory of Marxism (historical materialism) and science (pseudo-science) they promise a better world made up of division, hatred of the good and reverse-think.

In the past, the Church's control of the economy ensured that the average citizen could not live without having his savings constantly drained from him. His energy was taxed by the nobility, he was restricted from owning and using property and his work was given over to supporting his masters. It took capitalism to put a stop to it.

Today, the Alinsky Radicals and their financial supporters are selling short on America. They are looking for any pocket of wealth and seeking to drain that wealth from the average citizen into their own coffers. This is happening, just like it did in medieval times, without anyone realizing it.

Indeed, we are seeing the emergence of the new "nobility", the new owners of everything, the people who must be paid tribute so that average men can eke out a living in whatever way they, the masters, decide. These men work within the cracks of society, developing strategies that take advantage of men's fallibility, sneaking and hiding while the wealth of the average man is shoveled into their offshore accounts. These men buy politicians, pay protestors to vent fake outrage and block the streets, and they foster laws that keep them hidden and legally protected while they criminally meddle in our lives and launder our money.

There have essentially been two approaches that communists have used in order to advance a country toward socialism/communism/fascism. The first is the revolutionary approach and the second is the democratic approach. These two approaches have often been used concurrently depending upon the opportunities available and the depth of whatever crisis the left has created.

Marx countenanced a revolutionary approach bent on taking over a government through violent means. The justification for this was the realization by communists that the capitalists, because they had lots of money, did everything possible to maintain their control of the means of production. And since communism represented the next phase of the historical process, then it was proper to hasten the fall of capitalism.

The democratic approach involves incrementally making small coercive changes to government through legislation. These steps include regulations, re-distributive programs and other "social changes" that advance the power of government. This approach would accomplish change over time with the ultimate goal being a "nanny" state where the government manages the entire economy. The incremental approach, over time, brings the nation closer to full control. To spur these smaller moves, progressives keep inventing ways that capitalism has failed for which they recommend measures to "fix" these failings.

By using a utilitarian approach to economic evaluation, the

communists were able to appeal to the masses by first, showing the "damage" done to them by predatory capitalism and second, by promising to fix things through regulations that strangled the economy. By ensuring that capitalism was always blamed for the failure of regulatory policies, they were able to succeed politically and keep winning elections.

Progressive complaints against the so-called failures of capitalism were either poor economic analysis (due to prejudice against profits) or outright lies based upon a Marxist critique of capitalism. Generally, any real failures of capitalism were caused by government regulations.

Correct economic theory observes that all capitalist transactions are based upon people freely trading value for value. Mutually beneficial trades are, for the most part, honest. Combine these mutually beneficial transactions across a vast economy and you will find no systemic failures but an ever-improving economy as more and more people make better and better products to sell at lower and lower prices. This means that any claim that capitalism has failed is spurious and false. There is nothing to "fix" in capitalism and if there is a problem, the solution is freedom.

Marxism is the scourge of the world. Marx attempted to agitate the entire world against capitalism and in so doing he challenged and (to a large extent) destroyed the only system that meant hope for mankind. By relying on Christianity's disdain for profit seeking and property rights, he capitalized on some of the worst ideas in history and elevated envy and moral guilt into positions of power. Communism could never have existed without the morality of Christianity and the hatred of profit.

Today, we are at a crossroads. Those of us who have been

influenced by the ideas of the Enlightenment; as well as the "Second Renaissance" made possible by Ayn Rand, know that man needs individual rights and property rights. We are convinced that capitalism is the best alternative to the dictatorships of the Marxists and Alinsky Radicals. In fact, these Marxist groups are throwbacks, regressives, who are bringing back the tyrannies of the past rather than ushering in a new period of benevolence and freedom.

Many progressives are merely average people who think they are doing the right thing. Perhaps, as young people, they saw something wrong and blamed it on selfishness and decided that we had to stop people from being selfish. In fact, I was once like that. As a Catholic, I grew up thinking that selfishness and capitalism were enemies of the good (that I identified with "God"). I was taught that people should stop being selfish and start sacrificing for others – and that *this* was the only answer to world problems. That answer was encapsulated in the idea that, as Catholics, we need to work toward a world ruled by the "One True Religion". The words of our present Pope should prove informative in this regard.

I'm certain that most progressives today hold a version of this mindset. They may have started in life believing that sacrifice was the only way to create peace in the world. I know many liberals who are nice people; they just happen to advocate re-distribution without knowing the full meaning of it. They cringe when people like me call altruism evil and leftists devious. "They're just trying to make things better," is the response.

If it were only as easy as that, we wouldn't be in a world of massive government debt. That so-called "better" world is here and the Alinsky Radicals in charge are not nice people. Perhaps my liberal friends have not noticed the scandals, the deceptions, the fudging of economic statistics, the vote-buying, the outright lies, the stonewalling and the anti-capitalist vitriol that characterize today's "liberal" Alinsky Radicals.

These people mean their anti-capitalism. Their reaction to the Supreme Court ruling on "Citizens United" is a case in point. Their unwillingness to grant non-profit tax status to Tea Party groups is another. Their sending out onto the streets people who are willing to kill police officers is another. Their efforts toward gun control is another. We could go on forever about the "indications" that there is something sinister about what today's "liberals" are doing. For them, it doesn't take a village. It takes a shakedown.

If you think today's liberals are your father's liberals, you aren't looking at reality. You're holding so many contradictions and rationalizations that you have removed yourself from the realm of rational analysis. I too would like to think that we live in a wonderful world and that all is fine; that we are still free people doing our best. But then, I look at what I see. I know when I'm looking at criminals and liars. I don't hold contradictions and I'm not wearing blinders.

Alinsky Radicals Are Not Your Friends

Most progressives and communists do not think they are establishing a dictatorship. The progressives, especially, sometimes use the language of individual rights; they lay claim to practical "solutions" and insist they are fighting for the rights of people. They want you to think they are still advancing the cause of the American Revolution. They are fighting for the people, they tell us.

But the rights they are fighting for always require sacrifice on the part of productive citizens. This proves they are not freedom fighters but political agitators. They are members of a long line of "leftists" that get their inspiration and anti-capitalism from the children of Marxist communists. The veil was lifted in 1996.

In 1996, a book was published in France that caused a stir among European intellectuals. Entitled "The Black Book of Communism", this book sparked heated debate about the moral worth of communism and the tactics of a whole range of communist sympathizers that must certainly include, in our time, the Alinsky Radicals:

"What the Black Book of Communism succeeded in demonstrating is that Communism in its Leninist version (and, one must recognize, this has been the only successful application of the original dogma) was from the outset inimical to individual rights and human freedom. As Martin Malia stated in the foreword to the American edition: 'The communist regimes did not just commit criminal acts (all states do on occasion); they were criminal enterprises in their very essence: on principle, so to speak, they all ruled lawlessly, by violence, and without regard for human life.' In spite of its overblown rhetoric about emancipation from oppression and necessity, the leap into the kingdom of freedom announced by the founding fathers turned out to be an experiment in ideologically driven, unbounded social engineering. The very idea of an independent judiciary was rejected as 'rotten liberalism.' The party defined what was legal and what was not: as in Hitler's Germany, where the heinous 1935 Nuremberg Laws were a legal fiction dictated by Nazi racial obsessions, Bolshevism from the outset subordinated justice to party interests. For Lenin, the dictatorship of the proletariat was rule by force and unrestricted by any law. His famous reply to Kautsky speaks volumes about the true ethos of his ideology: 'The revolutionary dictatorship of the proletariat is rule won and maintained through the use of violence by the proletariat against the bourgeoisie, rule that is unrestricted by any laws'"[32]

"The class enemy had to be weeded out and destroyed without any mercy. Andrei Vyshinsky, Stalin's hysterical prosecutor in the Moscow show trials of the 1930s, carried this macabre logic to its ultimate consequences when he made the defendants' confessions the main argument for sentencing them to death. In other words, the presumption of innocence was replaced by a universalized presumption of guilt. As for the rhetoric of hatred, comparable to Goebbels's most insanely inflammatory speeches, this passage is worth quoting:

'Shoot these rabid dogs! Death to this gang who hide their ferocious teeth, their eagle claws, from the people! Down with that vulture Trotsky, from whose mouth a bloody venom drips, putrefying the great ideas of Marxism! Let's put these liars out of harm's way, these miserable pygmies who dare to dance around rotting carcasses! Down with

[32] *The Devil in History* by Vladimir Tismaneanu University of California Press, p. 30. Lenin quotes from Cohen *Bukharin* p. 133

these abject animals! Let us put an end once and for all to these miserable hybrids of foxes and pigs, these stinking corpses! Let their horrible squeals finally come to an end! Let's exterminate the mad dogs of capitalism, who want to tear to pieces the flower of our new Soviet nation! Let us push the bestial hatred they bear to our leaders back down their throats!'[33]

The idea that the brutalities of the communists were anomalous is quite common today. Yet, a case can be made that communists, socialists, progressives and radical leftists are a common group with common characteristics. Most defenders of communism, especially the progressives, virtually ignore these brutalities because their audience is made up of young people who never lived through those murderous times and they never crouched sleepless in their rooms waiting for a knock on the door. The result is that the atrocities of the communists, which far surpassed those of the Nazis, have gone relatively unnoticed, so much so that advocates of socialism can still worship the monsters of communism (such as Mao and Che) and kids today can proudly wear their t-shirts. The fact that the perpetrators of those monstrous atrocities are revered as men ahead of their time is a disgrace. As Professor Kors, discussing Hayak, reminds us:

"It is no accident of time or place that the concentration of power over all human life in a centrally planned society attracted and rewarded the aggressive, unscrupulous and demagogic who would attract around them the simultaneously submissive and ruthless. Central planning

---

[33] Vyshinsky quoted in Stephané Courtois, in "Crimes Terror, Repression," his conclusion to *The Black Book of Communism* (Cambridge, Mass,: Harvard University Press, 1999) p. 750, quoted by Vladimir Tismaneanu in *The Devil in History, Communism, Fascism, and some lessons of the Twentieth Century*, University of California Press, 2012

would bring forth leaders who took power, not as a necessary evil, but as an end in itself. Economic power over the whole life of other persons, Hayak judged, centralized as political power, created a society of slave masters and virtual slaves in which a leader's decisions about the good of the whole overrode all individualist ethics and law. In such a society, those limited by ethical prohibitions would flee power and, in Hayak's words, "those literally capable of everything" would rise to high positions under a ruler whose primary passion in life was to be obeyed. There were institutional and psychological reasons why socialism with authentic political power must lead to tyranny and cruelty."[34]

Yet, many socialists claim that earlier forms of socialism were wrongly practiced, and that true socialism is actually democratic, peaceful and benevolent. They dismiss the murders and atrocities and continue to preach the proud utopian future that will come when all men learn self-sacrifice and peace. They invoke Rousseau's social contract to make socialism into a system of supreme citizen participation. It is the "We" generation, after all.

The Black Book of Communism shows this premise to be a lie as Lenin's statement indicates. In fact, the gangsters of the Soviet Union were pragmatists who knew full well that their actions were about attaining power and control, not about the "workers of the world." It was not about creating a peaceful collective with gardens and flowers; rather it was about overthrowing the factory owners, seizing their wealth and taking over their factories. It was about theft.

The advocates of coercive government claim to base their actions upon their vaunted desire to help people. They glorify

---

[34] Socialism's Legacy – Lest we Forget, a lecture by Alan Charles Kors, The Clemson Institute for the Study of Capitalism

altruistic sacrifice and proclaim that their only goal is to make life better for those who have been victimized by society. The term "society" in this context means capitalist society. Their assumption is that there is something inherently exploitative in a society where "anything goes", where there is no control over the choices and actions taken by people. To them freedom means anarchy, exploitation and the victory of evil. By this view, the weak are most cruelly used for the pleasure of the strong – a statement commonly made by leftists.

These arguments, however, are not based upon experience. They are instead concocted for the sake of switching the tables on the capitalists, blaming freedom and capitalism for the very atrocities the left has brought to society. This has been proven by history and by the "Black Book of Communism".

The Alinsky Radicals are today's "Leninists" on the block. They use the common man like Lenin used the workers; as backdrops, photo ops and pure propaganda. Class warfare for them is a mere tool designed to wrest power from the corporations. Make no mistake about it, these gangsters want the same thing Lenin wanted, power and money.

The Alinsky Radicals demand blindness from their victims. They tell us, if only everyone would sacrifice for the whole, participate in society, be dedicated to working as hard as possible, then, and only then, can the system work. Then and only then, can we have abundance and make life enjoyable for everyone. It isn't about you, they want you to think. It is about others. We should live it, be it.

With this promise of a better future, given without proof, millions of people have said, "Yes". But what they said "Yes" to was a society of dedicated proletariats working out of love for humanity. They did not say "Yes" to brutality and murder.

Yet, they will have nothing to say when they find themselves among the "scoundrels", with a gun pointed at the backs of their heads.

When the Alinsky Radicals decide it is time to "clean up", you'll know you were a dupe and a slave all along. People always get the government they deserve.

The Unseen

There are consequences to the leftist calls for sacrifice. I call them "the unseen". Henry Hazlitt calls them the broken window fallacy and conservatives call them "unintended consequences." The unseen happens because leftists don't want you to see the consequences of their actions. It is as if they have mental blinders and they expect you to have them as well. These mental blinders help them block everything except the fiction, the magical world of "good" that is created by sacrifice. They don't want you to see what happens beneath the moral cover of the Alinsky Radicals.

First, leftists don't see that the middlemen in the altruist equation are not really nice people. Instead, they are people who see government as an opportunity to obtain wealth at little cost. They talk in pious platitudes about the value of sacrifice so they can skim off millions during the transfer of funds.

Secondly, the amount of money required for collective schemes is an ever-growing sum. There will never be enough sacrificing. Of this, you can be sure. As productive people go home each night, more tired than the night before; as they see more and more of their hard work going into a bottomless abyss, they will stop feeling a sense of euphoria from helping others.

Thirdly, they ignore the reasons for the decline in economic production and begin to look for scapegoats to blame for it. They judge any slowdown in production to be theft from the needy. The productive person cannot claim that he is being worked too hard or that it is unfair to ask so much of him. So he or she must bear the punishments, while the leaders increase their production quotas and the nation plunges into despair.

In order to maintain their higher living standards, the leaders must get the most production possible out of the workers. After a time, the coming utopia seems farther and farther away because the society is no longer providing enough production to maintain a vibrant economy. The amount slated for re-distribution increases but the tax revenues decline. To deal with this, more money is printed and this causes inflation. Returns continue to diminish. The workers are no longer enamored of the utopian dream that seems never to come. The harder the productive are required to work, the less production there is to re-distribute and the more the government must borrow. The economy verges on collapse.

But the leaders refuse to blame themselves. Quota slackers are punished and now called saboteurs. The ablest are suspected of being spies for a foreign enemy (which creates fear of a military invasion). In order to convince people of the "truth" of sabotage, they encourage citizens to inform on each other.

Now the disgraced former administrators are losing their jobs, benefits, homes, etc. Something must be done to stem the tide of decline. Some are jailed and, just to make a statement about the evil of sabotage, some are killed summarily. "Sabotage" has a price. None of this improves the economy because the critical players, the productive people, have been removed from the scene while others have become disenchanted over their "no win" situation.

As things continue to collapse, and more people begin to slack off, the middlemen themselves become the victims of political retribution, treachery and political revolts. If the old group is not brutal in maintaining power, a new group takes power and promises to make things work. The crimes of the old group are uncovered and show trials and executions ensue.

Some of the people are heartened as the new group tries to convince people they are good guys who won't treat the people as badly as the previous group had done. The cycle of sacrifice starts over, a temporary improvement makes it look like the new group is more efficient and a new generation of productive people are set up for the next fall. Propaganda and lies proliferate. This time, the suppression is hidden from sight and people are disappearing without notice. No one knows what happened to them but everyone knows what happened to them.

There is no way to make a re-distributionist society into a vibrant one. First, it takes wealth taken from those who produce it. Secondly, it eliminates the incentive to produce future wealth. These two simple facts have been unseen for millennia because the proponents of re-distribution have only pointed to the benefits going to the needy while ignoring the harm to the productive (who learn that it is easier and safer to join the ranks of the needy). They ignore the unseen, the consequences of their own policies. They ignore the immorality of re-distribution (forced charity).

The New Capitalist Radical

Against this backdrop of progressivism and the Alinsky Radicals, a new intellectual grass roots movement must be created to develop a strategy for advancing the ideas that will change the conversation. First and foremost, the four pillars of the progressive movement must be debated. These pillars are mysticism, altruism, collectivism and government coercion. However, discrediting these ideas must be accompanied with their corresponding solutions which are reason, self-interest, individualism and liberty.

Mysticism

The influence of mysticism on a free society is felt in the ideas that militate against reason. Mysticism is the view that knowledge is given to man from another dimension, communicated through intuition, scripture or revelation. In the case of the Alinsky Radicals, mysticism takes the form of a false metaphysics that asserts a historical inevitability (socialism) that has no relationship to reality.

One could write volumes on the fallacies mentioned above. The fundamental flaw in mysticism, regardless of the rhetoric, is that one can't get knowledge from a mere interpretation of future history. The unfortunate result is a fantasy and a false promise of better days that never come.

The mystics of progressivism don't understand that a secular society has no predictable fantasy. In fact, people focused on reality represent something new in the history of the world; the freedom of the mind to decide its own course without reference to a historical process. Reason is the source of individual rights, property rights and independent thinking, not some fictional Absolute Mind or historical promise.

Altruism

Yet, the secular world is not bereft of irrationality. Challenging the hold of mysticism on the mind of man, although a worthy goal, has not always resulted in complete liberation. The singular religious precept that secular philosophies did not challenge was primordial altruism. Many of modern philosophy's key secular intellects were men whose backgrounds were piously religious (Kant). Many of these men privately questioned the Church but kept their thoughts to themselves. Others openly wrote about their religious views and inserted them side by side with their secular views, insisting all along, that they were not challenging religion (Locke).

I have discussed altruism extensively in a previous chapter by that name. The point of *this* discussion is to suggest that altruism is the key concept that must, finally, be targeted by the New Capitalist Radicals.

Altruism is human sacrifice. As such, it cannot shed the evils and deceptions practiced during primordial sacrificial rites – all the way down to human sacrifice. As a ritual, altruism contains a disregard for human life and a willingness to sacrifice the individual for the sake of a better future that is impossible on those terms.

As a New Capitalist Radical, you must be clear that all falsehoods are evil; and this especially includes altruism. You must understand that there are only two ways to honor the rights of the individual; first, you must be certain that rights are inviolable and second, you must resist any effort to institute any form of human sacrifice including taxation, re-distribution, government regulation as well as government coercion against the mind and acts of man. Until and unless you understand these important principles you will never have an answer to the Alinsky Radicals and other progressives.

As Ayn Rand has written:

"But an honest man can cheat himself. His trusting innocence can lead him to swallow sugar-coated poisons — the deadliest of which is altruism. Americans accept it — not for what it is, not as a vicious doctrine of self-immolation — but in the spirit of a strong, confident man's overgenerous desire to relieve the suffering of others, whose character he does not understand. When such a man awakens to the betrayal of his trust — to the fact that his generosity has brought him within reach of a permanent harness which is about to be slipped on him by his sundry beneficiaries — the consequences are unpredictable."[35]

It is time to realize that our trust in altruism has been betrayed and the "harness" is about to be installed. Those who would make honest men into slaves can only do so by the consent of those men; by their agreement with the principle of altruism. For too long we have voted for and compromised with our executioners; those who would put chains upon us and make us into servants of the state. We must put a name to those individuals; they are radical leftists who have no regard for honest men and are intent on plunder; not on helping anyone.

"We cannot fight against collectivism, unless we fight against its moral base: altruism. We cannot fight against altruism, unless we fight against its epistemological base: irrationalism. We cannot fight against anything, unless we fight for something — and what we must fight for is the supremacy of reason, and a view of man as a rational being.

---

[35] Ayn Rand, The Ayn Rand Letter, Don't Let it Go

"These are philosophical issues. The philosophy we need is a conceptual equivalent of America's sense of life. To propagate it, would require the hardest intellectual battle. But isn't that a magnificent goal to fight for?"[36]

Collectivism

"Collectivism is the idea that the individual belongs, not to him but to the group or society of which he is merely a part, that he has no rights, and that he must sacrifice his values and goals for the group's "greater good." According to collectivism, the group or society is the basic unit of moral concern, and the individual is of value only insofar as he serves the group. As one advocate of this idea puts it: "Man has no rights except those which society permits him to enjoy. From the day of his birth until the day of his death society allows him to enjoy certain so-called rights and deprives him of others; not . . . because society desires especially to favor or oppress the individual, but because its own preservation, welfare, and happiness are the prime considerations."[37] [38]

Collectivism is the political expression of altruism. It is the virtual expropriation of the individual without his choice, and it is the demand that he sacrifice his life and product for the group. The evil of collectivism is found first, in the violation of individual rights that the collective imposes, and secondly, in the internal warfare it creates between individuals who find grievances in the system, and thirdly, in the mass genocide that is a common feature of the system.

---

[36] Ibid

[37] A. Maurice Low, "What is Socialism? III: An Explanation of 'The Rights' Men Enjoy in a State of Civilized Society," THE NORTH AMERICAN REVIEW, vol. 197, no. 688 (March 1913), p. 406.
[38] Individualism vs. Collectivism: Our Future, Our Choice, Craig Biddle, The Objective Standard, Vol. 7 # 1

There are many forms of collectivism, not the least of which is racism. As Ayn Rand indicates,

"Racism is the lowest, most crudely primitive form of collectivism. It is the notion of ascribing moral, social or political significance to a man's genetic lineage — the notion that a man's intellectual and characterological traits are produced and transmitted by his internal body chemistry. Which means, in practice, that a man is to be judged, not by his own character and actions, but by the characters and actions of a collective of ancestors."[39]

All forms of collectivism are essentially anti-mind and anti-man. There can be no valid argument for collectivism and the entire concept should be rejected completely by anyone advocating individual liberty. Indeed, the tenets of collectivism are an evil assault on the individual and a moral blot on the history of mankind.

Government Coercion

Coercion is the feature of government action that results from mysticism, altruism and collectivism. Coercion destroys reason and makes it impossible. It is essentially force exerted by the gun or the law. The coerced individual need not use his mind because government will make him do what it wants. And this destroys the ability of men to survive. The concept of individual rights, on the other hand, holds that any kind of coercion against a rights-respecting individual is immoral and should be prohibited from men's dealings; including and especially prohibited to the government.

---

[39] The Virtue of Selfishness, by Ayn Rand, "Racism" iBooks

These targets, mysticism, altruism, collectivism and government coercion must be the focus of any effort to discredit the Alinsky Radicals and all other leftists. They represent the worst ideas, the most immoral ideas, that have ever been offered to man throughout his entire history. Their source is tribalism, human sacrifice, despotism, force and hatred of man's mind. They must be resisted at all costs.

Rather than debate how much mysticism is ok, how much altruism is ok, how much collectivism we can allow, how much coercion is acceptable, our opposition to the Alinsky Radicals must have the power of "No", a complete rejection of these concepts. We must stop splitting hairs about issues of morality and especially morality in government and "Just say no" to these targets. Our goal should be to crush the Alinsky Radicals philosophically and politically; defeat them, disenfranchise them and reject them totally just like we rejected the Nazis and for the same reasons.

Ten Rules for New Capitalist Radicals

Every government program (from Cap and Trade, Obamacare, Fannie Mae, Freddie Mac, Green New Deal, Medicare for all, free college for all and more) can rightfully be considered to be a re-distribution program intended to take your money and give it to people who did not earn it. These programs are essentially money laundering schemes intended to make corrupt politicians, professional parasites (community organizers) and corrupt businesspeople rich using your money. It is based on government coercion; a violation of your individual rights.

During the Obama years, we saw the victory of the Alinsky Radicals; they thought their day had arrived. The champagne was being poured. They have you where they want you. They think they are smarter than you because they educated you and they know that they are finally free to expand the re-distributive state ad infinitum. They think there is no end to how much of your labor they can steal.

But there was a problem with the victory of Obama's trainees. They didn't really win; it was a deception. Obama did not run as an Alinsky Radical; he ran as a uniter and he promised to be inclusive of all people. When he started to rule, when he started to demand sacrifice and collective joining, he found out that the opposition to statism was stronger than he expected. To avoid it, he made sure he was out of town when the first massive Tea Party demonstrations began in 2009 DC. He pretended that nothing unusual had happened and acknowledged it only after the 2010 mid-term elections which he called a Democratic "shellacking". But, in large measure, he didn't change his promise of a "transformation" of society. The left has been seeking that same transformation ever since.

If we are to regain our freedoms, you must become a New Capitalist Radical. Each of you must be willing to metaphorically crush the Alinsky Radicals and rid the world of them forever; make them an afterthought in the struggle for liberty. Below is my attempt to develop *real* Rules for New Capitalist Radicals. These are my suggestions on how we can fight the savages and get rid of them.

1. Always argue from your basic premise – your individual rights - They have no right to take your money and give it to someone else. Every coercive measure limits your ability to thrive and steals your hard-earned money.

- Every government entitlement program is a form of re-distribution (theft) of your money.

- No one voted the government into dictatorial power – we should still expect them to honor the same Constitution that every other leader in this country has sworn to honor, no matter how much they hate it and want to overturn it.

- You have a right to earn a living and be happy.

- They have no right to take away your property.

- They have no right to regulate your economic actions.

- They have no right to destroy your freedom of speech or any other freedoms protected under the Constitution.

- Proper government is supposed to protect each and every citizen from the violation of his rights by the government.

- Capitalism is the implementation of individual rights economically.

- When the government violates individual rights, it destroys the ability of people to have free and peaceful commerce.

- Any government that violates individual rights is immoral and must be stopped or changed.

- Man survives by means of his mind. He must use reason in order to survive. Using reason is an individual decision. No one has a right to decide for a man what he should do when reason prescribes something else. Destroy freedom of action and you destroy society. You cannot have a moral society if you interfere with man's right to be free.

- It is offensive to say they have "no problem" "investing" your money. Spending is not investing. That they have "no problem" with it makes it your problem. They don't own your money.

2. Get them to accept your basic premise; if they don't then pronounce moral judgment and declare them unfit for debate. This moral judgment would be appropriate under the circumstances.

- Do they believe in individual rights? – Insist that they make a statement of their position - then show them how individual rights should be protected in any given issue.
- Don't accept "Yes, but…" arguments.

- It is your politician's job to ensure that the government does not violate your rights – it is not his or her job to lie to you about why or how the government should use your money to benefit anyone else.

- Do they protect the Constitution?

- Do they understand the Bill of Rights?

3. Never accept their basic premise which is force - Their basic premise is that coercive government has the right and responsibility to make you sacrifice for the sake of others. Whenever you challenge them on their basic premise, they will tell you that you are evil, selfish, in the pay of corporations, etc. This is wrong. Show how they are the advocates of dictatorship.

- They want you to feel guilty for living a moral life. They want to make you feel immoral if you do not go along with their wishes. Refuse to give in to the idea that force against people is a valid aspect of government..

- It is not proper that you be forced by government to provide your neighbor's government benefits. They do not have the right to force you to take care of your neighbor.

- "Morality ends where a gun begins." – Ayn Rand

- It is cruel to force a man against his will.

- You have a right to decide who gets your money. That is a private decision.

- Government is not entitled to care for any citizen with another citizen's money.

- It is immoral to make one man the slave of another. Re-distribution enslaves the productive person for the sake of the non-productive.

- Production does not take place in a vacuum…someone must decide to work hard and do well. What gives the government the right to invalidate that decision by means of force?

- Any government that decides to pick economic winners and losers is a fascist state.

- "Social Justice" is a euphemism for re-distribution and means expropriation and force against productive citizens. There is no "justice" with "social justice".

Mises explains (using the term "public welfare" for which "social justice" is a euphemism):

"But that Socialism alone has the public welfare in view can at once be denied. Liberalism (the advocacy of Laissez Faire Capitalism) champions private property in the means of production because it expects a higher standard of living from such an economic organization, not because it wishes to help the owners. In the liberal economic system more would be produced than in the socialistic. The surplus would not benefit only the owners. According to Liberalism therefore, to combat the errors of Socialism is by no means the particular interest of the rich. It concerns even the poorest who would be injured just as much by Socialism. Whether or not one accepts this, to impute a narrow class interest to Liberalism is erroneous. The systems, in fact, differ not in their aims but in the means by which they wish to pursue them."[40]

4. Always look them in the eye.
This method takes the moral high ground and puts them in their place. It communicates the certainty you have in your position. The honest person never flinches when facing evil.

5. Always defuse their argument – stay in reality and point out the unreality of their position.
A correct argument is based in reality and in consequences (the immoral leads to the impractical). Every form of re-distribution has unintended consequences that can often be identified by careful thought. Every government intrusion is justified by lies and distortions. Learn how to recognize them and how to defuse them.

- Read the writings of the Founding Fathers as well as good free market thinkers like Henry Hazlitt, Ludwig von Mises, Alex Epstein, Leonard Peikoff, Jaron Brook, Andrew Bernstein and Ayn Rand to name a few.

---

[40] Socialism by Ludwig von Mises, Liberty Classics Hardcover, Page 46

- Government coercion takes place whenever the government tries to prescribe for people what they should do.

- Government coercion is force. Force always replaces the individual's mind with the government's decision. This is immoral.

- Remember, good economic arguments expose the bad consequences that stem from the economic distortions brought about by government intervention. The moral argument is where you take a stand for your right to act in your own self-interest without interference from the government.

- All economic problems are caused by government interference in the marketplace…not by private decisions made by people trying to do the right things for themselves.

- When the government wants to "fix" an economic problem, always look for what they did to create the problem and then refuse their solution. That will fix the problem.

- Leave men free and they will solve their own problems.

6. Use the boycott.

Don't give them your money, don't give them your vote, don't give them an inch because they intend to rule, and they don't care what you think. Every statist politician must be disenfranchised and excised from the fabric of our society. We have assumed for too long that everyone is entitled to their opinion and we have given them the very platforms from which they seek our destruction. Boycott their contributors, their sponsors, their publishers and use the power of disenfranchisement whenever you can. Starve them out, call them out and give them no quarter.

7. Don't let them get away with logical fallacies. Reason is on your side. Below is a list of only the most common logical

fallacies. Study logic and know it thoroughly. You need your best weapons and they are ideas.

- Ad hominem – attacking the man rather than arguing the issue – also called ridicule or personal attack.

- Changing the subject – avoiding the issue or answering a question not asked.

- Equivocation – using the same word with more than one meaning in order to confuse the opponent

- Moral outrage – pretending that someone has said something morally reprehensible; sometimes call selective outrage or moralizing.

- Walking stick – threat of force.

- Circular reasoning – using the point you are trying to prove as part of your argument.

- Appeal to pity – engendering guilt by pointing to the suffering of others – this is not the issue. Your rights are the issue.

- Non sequitur – the conclusion does not follow from the argument

- Soliciting agreement – asking you if you accept their premise which is wrong – such as "You agree that it is right for the government to provide for the common good, don't you?" or "You agree that something has to be done about the poor, don't you?" The answer is "No, I don't agree."

8. Know the Constitution and understand the reasons for the Bill of Rights.

Especially, you should understand the principle of limited government; that a government should be prohibited from violating the rights enumerated in the Bill of Rights.

Progressives have struggled to invalidate the constitution – you should put them back on point and show people how the principle of individual rights is inviolable. Progressives also think they can interpret the constitution in any way that serves their particular political goal (such as to impeach Trump) by appealing to something the Founding Fathers said. Don't fall for this and attempt to discern the contradiction in their views.

You should internalize these arguments and make them part of your everyday living. Learn to recognize the expression of freedom and encourage it in others. Especially, know how to live your freedom, how to make it part of your successful living. That's what it is for.

9. Know the types of governments. Understand the basic premises of each type of government. Be an expert on proper government – just like the Founders.

- Limited government – a government limited to protecting individual and property rights. It is a government that bans force in society and only uses force to fight crime and fraud against otherwise free citizens.

- Statism - a political system where the state makes all decisions and assumes the right to control all aspects of life of the individual.

- Fascist state – a government of private property where the government coercively tells people how to manage their property.

- Socialist state – a government that owns the major industries and decides production quotas for the economy.

- Communist state – a government that owns all property and makes all economic decisions.

- Welfare state – a government that is based on re-distribution of income from the producers to the non-producers – it requires a coercive state.

- Coercive state – a government that takes upon itself the right to make whatever decisions it deems proper for the citizens and to enforce its decisions by threat of punishment.

- Mixed economy – an economy consisting of some regulation and some freedom – sometimes also called a fascist state.

- Oligarchy – a government ruled by a group or family of property owners with the ability to create monopolies that restrict competition in favor of the ruling elite.

- Republic – a government ruled by the people but forbidden to engage in any coercive activities. The government can only function in protection of rights with most officials elected and given only limited powers - sometimes called a limited government. A Republic selects people to leadership who are presumably the most deserving and judicious.

- Democracy – a government where majority decision rules in all areas including capital punishment for any reason. Coercive governments often use the cover of a "democracy" to engage in persecution of citizens who dissent.

- Theocracy - a nation where the government is a religion.

- Anarchy - a situation where there is no government.

- Plutocracy - a government where the wealthy rule - similar to an oligarchy.

- Tribal society - a society where a tribe rules all members.

- Collectivism - a political ideology where the collective makes all decisions and the individual is required to do the will of the collective.

- Capitalism - an economic system that is based on individual rights and individual autonomy.

- Totalitarianism - a political system where the rule of the government is total.

- Tyranny - a political system where the government controls society with brutal disregard for the rights of citizens.

- Individualism - an ideology that holds the individual as a sovereign agent.

- Nihilism - an ideology that holds there is no value for man to pursue.

10. Understand that the enemies of freedom require you to accept the false medieval premise that all profit is theft. They ridicule the profit motive as a basic assumption. So, their attacks on businesspeople, businesses, the workings of the marketplace, capitalism, corporate free speech, capital accumulation, interest earnings and other forms of profit are efforts to eliminate your right to your earnings. These attacks amount to prejudice and bigoted hatred of success and honest living. They want to justify their taking of your money for their own uses and envy is their basic motivation.

Statists assert without proof that there is no such thing as an individual decision and that all decisions and economic results are collective in nature and belong to the group. You must stand against the evil of this anti-man attitude and fight for the good inherent in making money. Fight for your decision to use your mind to survive and assert your right to be as successful as possible, to live the most affluent life possible and to be free of moralizing meddlers who claim the right to your money. If your mind created it, it is yours and you should keep it.

It takes intelligence, ingenuity, planning and hard work to create profits. Profits are a sign of your ability to survive. They are created, not stolen from anyone. They are good and you should be proud of your ability to live well. Never fall for the old wive's tale that profits should be a cause of guilt.

A final point to both Democrats and Republicans: Look around you. The infrastructure of our society, energy plants, roads, automobiles, central heating, air conditioning, processed foods, computers, cell phones, iPods and all the other conveniences of our lives are proof that freedom is both moral and it works. In fact, it works because it is moral; it enables survival and the creation of values. This is the essence of our society. Someone had the foresight to realize that freedom and moral living are compatible and that the result would be a strong people not merely able to survive but able to survive well, to enjoy life and to become better individuals. This is the legacy of our Founding Fathers. Forget all the revisionist history. These men were the height of human foresight and principled thinking.

The capitalism of the 19th century has added years of comfort to our lives (Imagine having to ride a horse from Indianapolis to Washington DC). The automobile is a value created by free people using their minds. Our genius comes from our freedoms; the very freedoms protected by the Constitution.

Our society, to the extent that it has capitalist elements, is a great argument for extending capitalism, growing it and institutionalizing freedom in all spheres. Our conveniences reveal, in tangible terms, the value of defending individual rights. And they show what a truly moral society can accomplish. Despite President Obama's criticisms, the free market does work in wonderful ways.

Hopefully, these ten "rules" are a start to getting our freedoms back. We've got to stop this absurd theft of our children's futures. I'd welcome any suggestions.

Debating the Left

For this chapter, I did a survey of some news stories that I found on various networks and observed what was being said by the left. When I heard something that exposed the left's strategy of deception, I played it back and then made note of the lie or contradiction. This chapter will help you identify what the left's strategy is doing to our country and how to counter it.

Defeating the Alinsky Radicals is a matter of knowing how they construct their arguments. Virtually all the arguments and positions that the radicals use have a common structure which we will identify. By knowing this structure, you can begin taking apart their arguments and defeating them intellectually. You should learn it, integrate it and internalize it. And once you do, you will know their gimmicks and discover that you are right.

A term I often use to describe leftist arguments is that a leftist routinely and habitually thinks in reverse. This creates a cognitive weakness for him or her. Leftists cannot understand reality because they see it in reverse. This happens because they cannot tell the truth. In order to create division in society, they must use the Big Lie technique and this technique, couched as truth, is actually a lie. For instance, one Big Lie is that capitalism has failed. Time after time, they tell us about a weakness in capitalism that causes problems for the economy. In order to propagate that idea, they must lie about capitalism and this leads them to advocate some form of coercion which causes the problems they blame on capitalism. The Big Lie is true in reverse. It is not capitalism that has failed but their coercive "solutions" for capitalism that have failed. They see reality in reverse.

In fact, progressives think that the tactic of the Big Lie is one of their strongest. They think it works for them to instill a different truth in the minds of the people they are trying to convince. They know they are lying, but, like the pragmatists they are, they think the tactic is an intelligent one and that it creates a different truth favorable to their views. Since to them, people create their own personal and economic realities (polylogism), then it doesn't matter if the idea repeated is the true or not, they are making it true by constantly repeating it and the people who start thinking it are also going to vote on its basis and so they too are creating a reverse reality.

I'm sorry to say that reality doesn't work that way. When you lie, you are not creating a different reality; you are propagating falsehoods and anyone who believes the lie is acting upon falsehoods. He or she is incapable of understanding reality at all. To operate on a false premise is to miss the mark when it comes to accurate thinking; the individual is creating inefficacy and incompetence in himself and this is why progressive solutions do not, in the end, create a better world. With so many people operating on false premises, they can only do things wrong. Thinking in reverse means being wrong. Such is our current state of affairs.

Tactic: The Big Lie

Goal: Divide human understanding over an important issue. To create an insurmountable divide between the leftist (good) and his opposition (individuals, capitalism and constitutional rights).	

Method: Create a false perception. Pretend that leftist solutions are practical solutions to real problems. Pragmatism is the refuge of the leftist who wants to avoid the appearance that his arguments are ideological.	
Means 1: Create a charge against someone that can't be proven or denied but repeat it so often it is taken as true – use altruism to induce guilt and tarnish the opponent.	
Means 2: Ignore the unseen consequences of leftist policies.	
Means 3: Ignore the truth and the real solution which is almost always capitalism.	

Example #1:
Michael Brown killing

Goal: Divide human understanding over an important issue. To create an insurmountable divide between the leftist (good) and the opposition (individuals, capitalism and constitutional rights).	The proponents of the idea that Michael Brown was killed because of systemic racism in the community divides the agitators and other members of the Ferguson, Mo community from those who are white and presumed to be racist. This is also racism against whites. The insistence on this narrative by the agitators will be resisted by people who do not accept the narrative and who know the evidence does not support that conclusion. This creates unnecessary anger, misunderstanding and a desire to do violence to those who disagree with the oft-repeated narrative of racism.

Method: Create a false perception. Pretend that leftist solutions are practical solutions to real problems. Pragmatism is the refuge of the leftist who wants to avoid the appearance that his arguments are ideological.	The untrue perception here is that racism is rampant and ever-present and that black people are right in hating American society especially capitalism.
Means 1: Create a charge against someone that can't be proven or denied but repeat it so often it is taken as true – use altruism to induce guilt and tarnish the opponent.	The charge is that America is an evil country and white people should be gotten rid of, or, at the very least, the rich people should be taxed more, the police should leave criminals alone – as a matter of right. Repeat the idea that Michael Brown was killed because he was black and repeat it often so many people will take to be a truism.
Means 2: Ignore the unseen consequences of leftist policies.	Ignored here is the discrimination and racism being directed at white people and proper government functioning which is sacrificed for the sake of criminals and gangsters seeking to take advantage of prostrate police departments and other proper governmental functions. The damage done to civil society is palpable including "white flight" and destroyed neighborhoods.
Means 3: Ignore the truth and the real solution which is almost always capitalism.	The real situation is that racism is a very minor problem compared to past days. In fact, a great deal of progress had been made and was being made until this fake outrage was ginned up for the sake of unifying the black (collectivist) vote against conservatives.

Example #2:
The Rich Get Richer

Goal: Divide human understanding over an important issue. To create an insurmountable divide between the leftist (good) and the opposition (individuals, capitalism and constitutional rights).	The divide here is between the rich and the poor to create more "need" among the poor and more guilt among the rich.
Method: Create a false perception. Pretend that leftist solutions are practical solutions to real problems. Pragmatism is the refuge of the leftist who wants to avoid the appearance that his arguments are ideological.	The untrue perception here is that the rich are rich at the expense of the poor. This is based upon the idea called "zero-sum" transactions in which every gain by one person is a loss to another. So, when a rich person creates a product in his factory that poor people need, such as a cell phone, the perception is that the poor person is impoverished while the rich person gets his (the poor person's) money. This creates envy and anti-capitalism.
Means 1: Create a charge against someone that can't be proven or denied but repeat it so often it is taken as true – use altruism to induce guilt and tarnish the opponent.	The charge is that America is an evil country and the rich should be gotten rid of; at the very least, they should have their property confiscated or their taxes raised.
Means 2: Ignore the unseen consequences of leftist policies.	This creates a sort of "looting" of the rich through re-distribution of the money rightfully earned by the rich. The poor are seen as victims and this causes them to think they need not work to their highest ability because they have already been cheated. The poor suffer from moral impoverishment because they are taught they do not have to work hard and society owes them something.

Means 3: Ignore the truth and the real solution which is almost always capitalism.	The truth is that every individual is responsible for his own success or failure and that is not the fault of the rich. There is no exploitation in a free society because everyone has an opportunity to educate himself, to work in whatever field he likes and to make his/her own decisions.

Example #3:
Gun Violence

Goal: Divide human understanding over an important issue. To create an insurmountable divide between the leftist (good) and the opposition (individuals, capitalism and constitutional rights).	The divide here is between gun-control advocates and law-abiding citizens using guns for sport and self-defense. By confounding their abilities to arrive at agreement, the left exacerbates the divide between them and seeks to criminalize legal ownership of guns – the goal is to take away the concept of self-defense and leave men defenseless in the face of government power.
Method: Create a false perception. Pretend that leftist solutions are practical solutions to real problems. Pragmatism is the refuge of the leftist who wants to avoid the appearance that his arguments are ideological.	The untrue perception is that legal gun ownership is what causes gun violence. This is based upon a deliberate misperception that gun violence is being done by legal gun owners. The left must maintain this view in order to eventually disarm gun owners so it can take over and exert power over individuals.

Means 1: Create a charge against someone that can't be proven or denied but repeat it so often it is taken as true – use altruism to induce guilt and tarnish the opponent.	The charge is that the Constitution prohibits the left from controlling guns and this causes gun violence. Guns and gun ownership (which enable self-defense) are wrongfully blamed for the crimes done by the criminal, mentally ill and the envious.
Means 2: Ignore the unseen consequences of leftist policies.	The unseen here is the cover that this argument gives to criminals. Criminals, including those in government, are getting guns outside of the law and this epidemic has caused a rise in gun violence. Additionally, many criminals do their crimes because they are taught to believe that society is unfair. The result of gun control among the law-abiding is an increase in gun violence by criminals who are the only ones armed.
Means 3: Ignore the truth and the real solution which is almost always capitalism.	The second amendment was intended to enable the law-abiding citizen to protect himself against government. As the government becomes more "legally" coercive, it creates dissatisfaction among honest citizens and feels it is being threatened by dissent against its coercive policies. A coercive government needs to disarm the honest citizen so it can continue being more coercive.

Example #4:
Structural Inequality

Goal: Divide human understanding over an important issue. To create an insurmountable divide between the leftist (good) and the opposition (individuals, capitalism and constitutional rights).	The divide here is between rich and poor using income disparities as justification to raise taxes and/or confiscate the property of the productive.
Method: Create a false perception. Pretend that leftist solutions are practical solutions to real problems. Pragmatism is the refuge of the leftist who wants to avoid the appearance that his arguments are ideological.	The untrue perception is that the "structure" of government and business is intent on keeping people poor. Also, racism is considered part of the structure. The solution, for the leftist, is central government that controls all of society. The growth of government as a provider of benefits and services became the solution that could bury capitalism and destroy the profit motive.
Means 1: Create a charge against someone that can't be proven or denied but repeat it so often it is taken as true – use altruism to induce guilt and tarnish the opponent.	The charge is that capitalism has caused structural racism and poverty because it does not serve the poor. Robber Barons were intent on gaining economic power in order to control markets and destroy competition. The result of capitalist exploitation was poverty and therefore capitalism was evil because it kept the poor languishing in poverty.

Means 2: Ignore the unseen consequences of leftist policies.	The unseen is that money infusions into poor neighborhoods are used to line the pockets of the politicians. This creates anger and distrust in the community against professional grievance mongers. Politicians did not serve the people but served themselves and used their power to shakedown corporations and threaten stock values that led to extortion, bribery and regulations.
Means 3: Ignore the truth and the real solution which is almost always capitalism.	The truth is that inequality is caused by the failure of government. Most politicians who represent poor neighborhoods have a vested interest in keeping the mantra of inequality going because it means more government spending and more unwillingness to work. Normal citizens play the role of professional grievance mongers and disrupt the community and reduce the ability of capitalist organizations to serve their customers.

Example #5:
Women's Rights

Goal: Divide human understanding over an important issue. To create an insurmountable divide between the leftist (good) and the opposition (individuals, capitalism and constitutional rights).	The divide here is women vs. men and women vs. capitalism using income disparities and claims of discrimination.

Method: Create a false perception. Pretend that leftist solutions are practical solutions to real problems. Pragmatism is the refuge of the leftist who wants to avoid the appearance that his arguments are ideological.	The untrue perception is that capitalism structurally tends to discriminate against women and men are generally biased against women
Means 1: Create a charge against someone that can't be proven or denied but repeat it so often it is taken as true – use altruism to induce guilt and tarnish the opponent.	The charge is that capitalism and gender bias harm women in the same ways racism harms blacks. The solution is for government to force corporations to treat women fairly and for government to protect "reproductive rights".
Means 2: Ignore the unseen consequences of leftist policies.	The unseen here is the fact that capitalism is based solely on serving the customer and decisions must be based upon what is good for the business not individuals who are appropriating special privileges for themselves. Generally, capitalism pays people for their level of production. It makes no difference whether they are men or women. Production matters; not gender.

| Means 3: Ignore the truth and the real solution which is almost always capitalism. | What is sometimes termed "discrimination" or "gender bias" is nothing more than a measurement of the individual's contributions to the profits of the business. There is no gender bias in companies run by most owners who only want their businesses to succeed. If discrimination actually exists, those business owners should be dealt with by the free market which generally does not want to do business with unfair managers. The free market has self-correcting features. Managers who make bad decisions negatively affect the profit-making ability of the company in a negative way and eventually lose their jobs. This is true of racist business owners as well. |

Example #6:
Immigration

Goal: Divide human understanding over an important issue. To create an insurmountable divide between the leftist (good) and the opposition (individuals, capitalism and constitutional rights).	The divide here is immigrants (mostly from Central America) and the American people many of whom have no problem with legal immigration.
Method: Create a false perception. Pretend that leftist solutions are practical solutions to real problems. Pragmatism is the refuge of the leftist who wants to avoid the appearance that his arguments are ideological.	The untrue perception is that Americans hate immigrants who are mostly Hispanic

Means 1: Create a charge against someone that can't be proven or denied but repeat it so often it is taken as true – use altruism to induce guilt and tarnish the opponent.	The charge is that Americans are xenophobic and ethno-phobic and want to protect jobs over allowing people to come here to work.
Means 2: Ignore the unseen consequences of leftist policies.	The unseen is that unions and government have a pernicious influence on wages and tend to force them higher. Government prints too much money and this drives prices of consumer goods up and makes money less valuable. Governments are forced to hire cheap labor in order to stay in business but onerous immigration policies force people to come here to take low-paying jobs. Politicians on both sides of the aisle use the issue as a political football to gain votes from those people who want to discourage "illegal" immigration. There is no such thing as an illegal person.
Means 3: Ignore the truth and the real solution which is almost always capitalism.	This is not a racist country. People who want to come here for jobs and a better life are dropped into this mix and used for political purposes.

Example #7
Kavanaugh Hearings

Goal: Divide human understanding over an important issue. To create an insurmountable divide between the leftist (good) and the opposition (individuals, capitalism and constitutional rights).	The divide here is between left and right. The Democrats want you to think that they are the "good guys" and anything they do to thwart the "bad guys" is appropriate because supposedly only the left represents America.

Method: Create a false perception. Pretend that leftist solutions are practical solutions to real problems. Pragmatism is the refuge of the leftist who wants to avoid the appearance that his arguments are ideological.	The untrue perception is that any conservative or Republican is a monster who would do anything such as lie, cheat, steal, engage in wanton sex and objectify women. First they assume, tell the world what they assume and then they look for any evidence for their assumption. If there is no evidence, they will manufacture it and spread it far and wide.
Means 1: Create a charge against someone that can't be proven or denied but repeat it so often it is taken as true – use altruism to induce guilt and tarnish the opponent.	The charge is that Brett Kavanaugh was a sexual predator as an adult and as a high school boy attending sex parties.
Means 2: Ignore the unseen consequences of leftist policies.	The unseen is that there are no facts whatsoever that even hint at the possibility that Kavanaugh was a sexual predator as a high school student or adult. The left ignores this truth in favor of bias and prejudice against Kavanaugh because he is a conservative.
Means 3: Ignore the truth and the real solution which is almost always capitalism.	Kavanaugh is not a sexist or sexual predator. This attack tells us more about the left and their principles than it does about Brett Kavanaugh.

Example #8
Trump Impeachment

Goal: Divide human understanding over an important issue. To create an insurmountable divide between the leftist (good) and the opposition (individuals, capitalism and constitutional rights).	The divide here is between left and right. The Democrats want you to think that they are the "good guys" and anything Trump does reflects his corruption. Their proof? Trump is a business person so he must be corrupt. Capitalism is corrupt and so all they have to do is find the evidence; and, as usual, even if they invent the evidence, people will believe it.
Method: Create a false perception. Pretend that leftist solutions are practical solutions to real problems. Pragmatism is the refuge of the leftist who wants to avoid the appearance that his arguments are ideological.	The untrue perception is that any conservative or Republican is a monster who would do anything such as lie, cheat, steal, engage in wanton sex and objectify women. But, in Trump's case, it is even more true.
Means 1: Create a charge against someone that can't be proven or denied but repeat it so often it is taken as true – use altruism to induce guilt and tarnish the opponent.	The charge is that Trump is a crook who threatens everything the left has built up in terms of government programs, regulations, government contracts, crime and re-distribution as well as money laundering are without a doubt being threatened by Trump who must be gotten rid of by any means necessary..
Means 2: Ignore the unseen consequences of leftist policies.	The unseen is that Trump's policies, on the whole, have been good for the country and the left ignores this truth in favor of getting rid of Trump.
Means 3: Ignore the truth and the real solution which is almost always capitalism.	Trump is not a corrupt politician. While running for office, he promised to restore American values. This attack tells us more about the left and their principles than it does about Donald Trump.

If one wants to enter the discussion over the numerous class warfare divisions created by the left, one must take those arguments to the core; to the divisions that the left has used to divide society. For instance, Marx knew that in order to defeat the powerful capitalists he had to engender moral outrage against the capitalists in the minds of the factory workers and the poor.

This division was not a natural division, but one based initially on religious premises grounded in hatred of the rich and other merchants. When I say Marx based his arguments on religious premises, I am referring to his appropriation of Hegel's metaphysics and taking it upon faith, the assumption that it is true.

Marx ignored the truth that during the capitalist era, some of the "poor" were moving into the middle class while others were using capital to create new businesses and industries. But more than anything, it was the attitude that the rich were to be hated and envied that justified cruel treatment of them. Marx merely took advantage of this common attitude in order to further separate rich and poor in the same way that the Alinsky Radicals are doing today.

Yet, the solution to poverty is not expropriation of the property of the rich but "real" capitalism, freedom, individual rights and the Bill of Rights. Capitalism led to moral living and the possibility of happiness for people who adhered to the concept of economic liberty.

The Alinsky Radicals and the New Capitalist Radicals must always be political enemies because they want to establish opposite principles. The Alinsky Radicals use the evil tactics of divide and conquer while the Capitalist Radicals, for the most part, adhere to reason as the defender of freedom.

We need to get it straight that the left does not want things to get better; they want things to get worse so they can blame the consequences of their own policies on their political enemies. They want to escape culpability for the failures of socialism and they want to use those failures as an indictment of their opposition. We must stop them from doing this just like a police officer stops traffic.

Defeating the Arguments

In the USA, speech is free, but not all speech is good. Some of it is deliberately deceptive. Some speech is wrong or untruthful. Some is deliberately harmful.

It is generally thought, within leftist circles that winning an argument is not about having the best argument but about winning through the appeal to the emotions of people. By taking the position of the ignorant person and appealing to his emotions, the left plans to establish its utopia.

This view assumes that "the right" is made up of evil actors intent on exploiting and conquering the ignorant masses against their wills.

I have selected three leftist individuals for observation. These individuals are highly intelligent and verbally eloquent. They apparently have carefully studied their arguments and they are able to earn a living by pontificating on important issues from the perspective of their ideological purpose.

These individuals are Richard Goodstein, Marie Harf and Chris Hahn.

Richard Goodstein

Goodstein Example #1
Political Bias in Muller Probe

Goal: Divide human understanding over an important issue. To create an insurmountable divide between the leftist (good) and the opposition (individuals, capitalism and constitutional rights).	"This whole business about Peter Strozk's text messages is yet another distraction. Donald Trump should thank his lucky stars that the FBI existed. He would not be in the White House but for James Comey having given his press conference on July 5th sent that letter on October 28th and making no reference whatsoever to what the intelligence community knew which was that the Russians were trying to help Trump win, nothing, not a word, so for him and frankly his party members now to be screaming bloody murder about the FBI is just a bit much."
	Rule #10: 'If you push a negative hard enough, it will push through and become a positive.' This is the idea that if you repeat often enough the idea that the Trump campaign worked with the Russians to win, that people will believe it. The Dems pushed this unproven assertion for almost three years, and as we see by the segment on Fox News, Richard Goodstein is an expert at the Rules for Radicals.

	The divide here is between Democrats and Republicans. The Democrats want you to think that the administration worked with the Russians so you will think the Republicans, and especially, Trump won the election through subterfuge. Their proof? Trump is a business person so he must be corrupt. Capitalism is corrupt and so all they have to do is find the evidence; and, as usual, even if they invent the evidence, people will believe it.
Method: Create a false perception. Pretend that leftist claims are always correct. Pragmatism, bold leaps and political risks are the refuges of the leftist who wants to avoid the appearance that his arguments are ideological.	The untrue perception is that any conservative or Republican is a monster who would do anything such as lie, cheat, steal, engage in wanton sex and objectify women. But, in Trump's case, it is even more true.
Means 1: Create a charge against someone that can't be proven or denied but repeat it so often it is taken as true – use a constantly repeated charge to induce guilt and tarnish the opponent.	The charge is that Trump is a crook who threatens everything the left has built up in terms of government programs, regulations, government contracts, crime and re-distribution as well as money laundering are without a doubt being threatened by Trump who must be gotten rid of by any means necessary..
Means 2: Ignore the unseen consequences of leftist policies.	The unseen is that Trump's policies, on the whole, have been good for the country and the left ignores this truth in favor of getting rid of Trump.
Means 3: Ignore the truth and the real solution which is almost always capitalism.	There is no evidence Trump colluded with the Russians. This attack tells us more about the left and their principles than it does about Donald Trump.

Marie Harf

Harf Example #1
Giving ISIS Jobs

Goal: Divide human understanding over an important issue. To create an insurmountable divide between the leftist (good) and the opposition (individuals, capitalism and constitutional rights).	"We're killing a lot of them, and we're going to keep killing more of them. ... But we cannot win this war by killing them," department spokeswoman Marie Harf said on MSNBC's "Hardball." "We need ... to go after the root causes that leads people to join these groups, whether it's lack of opportunity for jobs, whether --"
Method: Create a false perception. Pretend that leftist claims are always correct. Pragmatism, bold leaps and political risks are the refuges of the leftist who wants to avoid the appearance that his arguments are ideological.	Alinsky Radicals see every issue as a sociological issue that blames capitalism for some failure. Here the assumption is that there is a reason why murderous terrorists behead people and it is because society (capitalism) does not give them jobs. It turns the criminals into victims of capitalism or society and fosters the idea that something should be done for men who do bad things because it really isn't their fault. It is our fault.
Means 1: Create a charge against someone that can't be proven or denied but repeat it so often it is taken as true – use a constantly repeated charge to induce guilt and tarnish the opponent.	The charge is that our society is doing something wrong to take care of peoples' "issues", that we must examine ourselves in order to understand why terrorists kill people. This is the same thought process that blames society for the criminals who rob and murder people in the USA. Society must give them opportunities and it is our fault that they rob and kill.

Means 2: Ignore the unseen consequences of leftist policies.	The unseen is that the people who work hard every day and create products and services are invisible. We should focus policy, not on the people who have chosen to work hard but on those who haven't. This is a backward strategy that avoids focusing on what makes productive people possible; which is freedom and individual initiative.
Means 3: Ignore the truth and the real solution which is almost always capitalism.	What societies beset by radical Islamism lack is freedom. The governments of those societies lack a sense of understanding that society must set up checks against murder and criminality and this is not done through government programs or charity; it is done by a justice system that knows the difference between citizenship and criminality. Alinsky radicals tend to focus on the criminals and using them for the sake of establishing social goals, technocracy and social manipulation of the productive for the sake of the unproductive.

Chris Hahn

Chris Hahn full one-on-one interview

Hahn Example #1
Gun Control

Goal: Divide human understanding over an important issue. To create an insurmountable divide between the leftist (good) and the opposition (individuals, capitalism and constitutional rights).	"I think we've got a gun culture in this country. We've got a Congress that doesn't want to do anything about it. I suspect that Donald Trump is not tied to the NRA as Paul Ryan and some of his members in the House and many of the members in the Senate, and I would like to see the President propose sensible gun solutions because I think the President can appeal to many parts of the country that many progressives for years won't be able to and I think that the President understands that something needs to be done and I'm hoping to God that over the next couple of weeks he proposes something that can break through and change this gun culture that is killing so many."
Method: Create a false perception. Pretend that leftist claims are always correct. Pragmatism, bold leaps and political risks are the refuges of the leftist who wants to avoid the appearance that his arguments are ideological.	Alinsky Radicals see every issue as a sociological issue that blames capitalism for some failure. Here Hahn is trying to separate Trump from his own followers, playing a psychological game of division, trying to get into his head, so to speak, and scare him into doing what Hahn wants him to do. He senses (an earned) weakness in Trump and hope he can turn him to the liberal position which is to take a position against the 2nd Amendment and the NRA.

Means 1: Create a charge against someone that can't be proven or denied but repeat it so often it is taken as true – use a constantly repeated charge to induce guilt and tarnish the opponent.	The charge is that our society is doing something wrong by having a "gun culture". Here is the Big Lie of the left, repeated constantly and drummed incessantly in order to make Americans feel guilty for defending their rights. Hahn wants to "guilt" all Americans so he can disarm them. Americans are gun-toting killers intent on using guns to kill people. He ignores the truth that there is a difference between criminals and people who use guns to defend themselves against the criminals. The left will repeat the charge forever until people eventually will start believing that there is such a thing as a lawless "gun culture."
Means 2: Ignore the unseen consequences of leftist policies.	The unseen is that the people who kill people with guns are criminals. By connecting law-abiding people with criminals, the left ignores the fact that they are actually liberating criminals and giving them a license to kill. By waging a war against law-abiding Americans, they are liberating the criminals and using them to help sow division, weakness and nihilism. The left is liberating destruction of the property of the law-abiding people which is their goal.
Means 3: Ignore the truth and the real solution which is almost always capitalism.	Americans are free people and it is their freedom that the left is trying to take away. The solution is always to defend freedom and individual rights and the left, as the destroyers of freedom and rights are destroying society.

Conclusion

This book is about starting a new radicalism that embraces the most successful, fair and proper system of government ever devised by the mind of man. That system is virtually the same system as devised by the founds of the United States government. This government provided an ingenious limited government that enabled liberty.

In a sense, then, the New Capitalist Radical is not merely a capitalist; but an advocate of a limited government that protected individual rights and fostered checks and balances and separation of powers. It was, as has often been observed, a government of laws and not of men.

Subsequent books on the topic of liberty will explore other factors in the struggle to create a proper society. This volume is the first volley, a suggestion on how to bring about liberty and individual rights by identifying and eliminating the enemies of liberty. Subsequent volumes will drill down into other factors that can help justify and bring about a proper, free and prosperous society. We have just begun to fight.

I'd like to make clear that my position is not on the right and neither is it on the left. Both left and right today are inconsistent in their advocacy of man's rights. Both have elements in their philosophies that violate individual rights. For the left, that violation occurs primarily in the economic realm where the rights of individuals to engage in trade is severely limited and proscribed by leftist technocrats who think they know what the ends of society should be and who have no problem using coercion (force) to bring it about. For these people, the end justifies the means and the result of this policy is, in the long run, dictatorship.

The right, on the other hand, violates individual rights when it comes to the right of a woman to protect her body and make decisions about her reproductive choices. The right would also, eventually, impose the Ten Commandments upon all of society which would lead, in the long run, to dictatorship.

I am opposed to both groups and advocate for capitalism which fosters a secularized form of individual rights where no individual or government has a right to impinge on the personal choices of any individual and any peaceful association he might join. This freedom applies in all matters and liberates all choices of the individual so long as he peacefully respects and acknowledges the similar rights of all other men. This system is built upon reason and the sanctity of the human mind. It exerts no effort to mold or interfere in the thinking derived from the free mind and it supports and protects the right of the free mind to think as it will and the right of the free individual to make decisions about his own life.

A good analogy for the New Capitalist Radical is that of a highly trained soldier. When a soldier fights against an enemy, he does not philosophize on the battlefield. His philosophizing is done before the battle during his training. He seeks to understand his enemy and learn why he is evil. He asks himself if the enemy deserves to die, and once he has considered these issues, he defines his purpose as a soldier. That purpose is to do whatever he can to destroy the enemy by any means possible. As a soldier, he knows that he may die; he may even be defeated; but he trains himself so he can be a successful killer of evil and he plans to enjoy a good life once that enemy is removed from the scene. As long as he is a solder, it is sufficient for him, if he has done an adequate job of training himself, that he sets his mind to his task of killing the enemy.

In a sense, the New Capitalist Radical is an intellectual soldier. He doesn't fight his enemy on the field of battle but on the field of the intellect. He wins over his enemy when his ideas have prevailed and been found to be reasonable and true. In this book, I hope I have helped you define the intellectual enemy of society and convinced you of his evil. I hope now you have decided that the Alinsky Radical must be politically destroyed.

It is my hope that people, particularly young people, will begin to question the tenets of collectivism, altruism and re-distribution. These ideas are the foundations of the worst actions that men can engage against one-another. I encourage you to learn as much as you can about these negative concepts and do all you can to understand why they are evil. This knowledge will help you in preparing yourself for the battle. It will teach you how to identify collectivism when it rears its head and it will prepare you to fight and defeat that enemy so it can no longer harm and devastate people.

Capitalism is the solution to all economic problems, just as free choice and reason are the solutions to all moral problems. Capitalism has no nation. Capitalism has no religion. Capitalism has no race and no gender or sexual orientation. Capitalism is the refuge of those seeking fundamental rights. It has no group, no collective. It is based upon individual self-reliance, freedom of action and individual rights.

Capitalism offers the way of solving all human problems because it liberates logic, reason and innovation. Capitalism is the idea that men should be free to make their own decisions without interference from other men or governments. It is the essence of fairness and goodwill.

The lies told about capitalism are legion and it is time to question these lies for what they are; an effort to steal the energy and work of honest men and women for the sake of the dishonest. Since the advent of progressivism, a constant stream of charges have been made against capitalism, most of which sought to institute controls and restrictions on the free trade of honest men. To understand this, I urge you to read the economic writings of Ayn Rand, Ludwig von Mises, Henry Hazlitt and others in order to see that these charges against capitalism are false.

Our enemy, the Alinsky Radicals, armed with false arguments, have every intention of winning politically. They want to seize the instruments of power and use them to milk your energy and your values until there is nothing left. They hope to be the "last man standing" in this elaborate "conspiracy" of the left to bring you down, to bring society down and to bring freedom down. Some of them may have nice smiles and conduct themselves honorably; but the Alinsky Radical is not a nice person. He needs to be put in his place upon the dust heap of history.

Leftism is irrational, illogical and regressive. Once we learn this, we will know that the true, historical solution to human problems is not socialism but capitalism. Capitalism is the suffrage movement, the movement for man's rights. It is the movement that fights for the individual.

A right is freedom of action and capitalism fights for complete freedom of action. This freedom acknowledges the fact that you must use reason in order to solve human problems and make a living. This fact alone is the fundamental truth that the advocates of capitalism have known and lived by. It supports the idea that a proper society protects and fights for freedom. And it is this very fact that the Alinsky Radicals and all leftists have sought to deny.

Yet, the end of the Alinsky Radicals is only the beginning of the struggle for freedom. Once the left is defeated, a host of right wing groups and organizations will rise up to pursue theological goals. They will try to impose religious principles, demand an end to abortions (which would violate the individual rights of women) and reintroduce God as the source of knowledge. These goals will give rise to a host of radicals that will be just as bad and just as oppressive as are the Alinsky Radicals.

The New Capitalist Radical will avoid defaulting to religious tyranny and will continue to champion individual rights, meaning the rights to speech, thought, self-defense and association.

The New Capitalist Radical will defend morality; a morality of freedom for the individual to make his own choices, not merely the freedom to believe but, more than this, the freedom to know. The freedom to know means that men should be free to think logically and scientifically and to follow knowledge and science for man as their guide. Certainly, men should be free to practice their religion so long as they don't seek to impose it on others. The New American Freedom is true freedom to think and to rely on one's own thinking.

Capitalism is the only political/economic system that makes a connection between a man's purpose, his values and his moral code. This connection makes capitalism the only proper system. Any thinking individual who understands how man survives will work to establish the kind of political system necessary to ensure his survival. He must inevitably fight for capitalism and he must fight capitalism's enemies; mysticism, altruism, collectivism and coercion.

In this book, I don't ask for faith. I ask for "premise-checking", critical thinking and a refusal to be bamboozled by liars who claim they are the only ones who care for people. Such liars offer only one solution to the problems of society: force. Our Founders had it right: man's struggle is the struggle for freedom and this brings values and values bring good living.

Welcome to the world of the New Capitalist Radical. Welcome to your freedom and your prosperity.

Other books by Robert Villegas

Title	Amazon Link
Crushing the Alinsky Radicals ISBN 978-1512172978	http://amzn.to/2rXPCyG
How to Write a Sponsorship Proposal ISBN 978-1517181642	http://amzn.to/2rJeWJg
Poems for the Stage: A Love Story ISBN 978-1519752000	http://amzn.to/2rORmdV
Adam Reborn – A Short Play ISBN 978-1516942374	http://amzn.to/2rOKr4O
Poetic Prose and Poetry ISBN 978-1516952113	http://amzn.to/2rDxxWo
Individualism ISBN 978-1518810138	http://amzn.to/2oVDP1u
Bob and Bobbie: A Korean War Story ISBN 978-1523924684	http://amzn.to/2oYlJev
The Boy Who Stood Alone ISBN 978-1516886456	http://amzn.to/2q1jWoh
Behind the Ritual Mask ISBN 978-1517752583	http://amzn.to/2qeG9lT
The Raven Haired Girl ISBN 978-1515253457	http://amzn.to/2plv3FK
The Biggest Mistakes in History ISBN 978-152369307	http://amzn.to/2qpaWd5
The Battle of the Sexes ISBN 978-1519147172	http://amzn.to/2p1w4E2
The Age of Selfishness ISBN 978-1517540371	http://amzn.to/2qsyYXm
Finding Sponsors Forms Book ISBN 978-1539566540	http://amzn.to/2pTyab8
The Libertarian Party versus Liberty ISBN 978-1539557531	http://amzn.to/2pUfQAT
Domitian: The Final Messiah ISBN 978-1542352215	http://amzn.to/2phfULM
The Conservative's Dilemma ISBN 978-1523416431	http://amzn.to/2qXK1YZ
The Secular Ten-Step Program Workbook ISBN 978-1539397785	http://amzn.to/2pGRx5v

The World's First Drunk: With Counselor's Talking Points ISBN 978-1539406938	http://amzn.to/2r6pCRA
Alcoholism and Addiction – A Secular Ten-Step Program ISBN 978-1539315346	http://amzn.to/2q8eQsB
The History of Altruism ISBN 978-1530844135	http://amzn.to/2r6Lplw
Website Development Methodology ISBN 978-1517463717	http://amzn.to/2r8IlM3
Adam Reborn – A Short Play and Adam Rayberne – A Short Story ISBN 978-1517417857	http://amzn.to/2qkBoXo
Finding Sponsors for Sport and Entertainment ISBN 978-1517362041	http://amzn.to/2pS31U8
The Art of Sponsorship ISBN 978-1537185415	http://amzn.to/2rmOBgK
Submitting Your Sponsorship Proposal Online ISBN 978-1537596167	http://amzn.to/2rezs3C
Unkilling Jesus ISBN 978-1517374467	http://amzn.to/2qvF9ZP
The Sport Sponsor Handbook ISBN 978-1516989928	http://amzn.to/2pQzEX3
Poems for the Stage: The Man at the Computer ISBN 978-1519752000	http://amzn.to/2rB6h7w
The REAL Purpose-Driven Life ISBN 978-154428055	http://amzn.to/2qlF994
The Values and Purpose Workbook ISBN 978-1544638324	http://amzn.to/2qRJerZ
Is this the Face that Launched a Thousand Ships? ISBN 978-1544680200	http://amzn.to/2qPu0Dk
The World's First Drunk – Patient Version ISBN 978-1539407195	http://amzn.to/2r0EBfr
The Hospitality Event Planning Handbook ISBN 978- 1516958375	http://amzn.to/2s3Xf3f
Has Capitalism Failed? ISBN 978-1534700048	http://amzn.to/2rOzTlx
The Lost Poems ISBN 978-1544963310	http://amzn.to/2rUCKtj

About Robert Villegas

Robert Villegas is an Arizona Author specializing in fiction, romance, theater, religion, politics and philosophy. He was born in South Texas (Weslaco) but raised in Indiana. He is Hispanic-American but American in every sense of the word. He has spent a lifetime in the business world as a UPS executive and also worked in locations all over the United States and Europe. He is an Army veteran who served as a telecommunications specialist in the 7th Infantry Division in Camp Casey, Korea. He was educated in Indiana and earned a Degree through the University of the State of NY (Albany) via an external degree program. He is divorced with three grown children and three grandchildren.

Alcoholism and Addiction – the System

These four books comprise a system that can be used by both patients and counselors who are battling Alcoholism and Addiction. Based upon Mr. Villegas's own system developed during his struggle against alcoholism, this system includes:

Alcoholism and Addiction – A Secular Ten-Step Program

This groundbreaking book offers a secular approach to alcoholism unlike that offered by Alcoholics Anonymous. We recommend that every individual going for alcohol and drug-abuse counseling be given a copy of this book which contains the workbook and the two versions of The World's first drunk. http://amzn.to/2md6R9w $3.45 Kindle $11.95 softcover

The Secular Ten-Step Program Workbook

This booklet covers the program developed by Mr. Villegas. It is designed as a workbook with blank spaces for the patient to write his own thoughts as he takes each of the ten steps. Order one copy for each patient in counseling. http://amzn.to/2lrHimS $4.49 Kindle $6.95 softcover

The World's First Drunk – With Counselor Talking Points

This booklet is designed for the counselor as he works with patients during individual or group therapy. It contains helpful tips on discussing the life story of the man who invented alcohol. Order one copy for each patient in counseling. http://amzn.to/2l446Wr $2.99 Kindle $5.95 softcover

The World's First Drunk – Patient Version

This version of the short story contains empty spaces where the patient can answer questions about the life story of the man who invented alcohol. Order one copy for each counselor. http://amzn.to/2ldxBGb $2.99 Kindle $5.95 softcover.

www.robertvillegas.com

Business Books by Robert Villegas

These four books by Robert Villegas comprise some of the business books that he has written. As an executive working for several companies, he was able to develop these methods that will help anyone seeking to excel in the business world. These books are:

How to Be a Great Employee – and a Greater Manager

You cannot be a great manager without first being a great employee. And this is something that requires learning, experience and attitude. The attitude comes from you but the learning and experience you should acquire through diligent study and practice. http://amzn.to/2BqdG2i $3.99 Kindle $8.95 softcover

SWOT Analysis Supercharged

A SWOT Analysis is an objective look at the internal and external elements of your organization that impact your success or lack thereof. If done diligently, you will always have a handle on what you need to do to improve season after season. http://amzn.to/2BCAWYx $3.99 Kindle $6.95 softcover

The Five-Module Call Center Training System

The Five-Module Call Center Training System is designed to assist the Call Center Team Leader in helping his employees quickly upgrade their skills to an acceptable level. http://amzn.to/2B3Svj1 $3.99 Kindle $5.95 softcover

Website Development Methodology

Effective strategic marketing requires the ability to differentiate the website development organization and its deliverables from those of the competition. http://amzn.to/2DnYMqh $2.99 Kindle $12.95 softcover.

www.robertvillegas.com

The REAL Purpose-Driven Life
After centuries of being told that it is not about you, it is time to set the record straight. You are a unique individual and your goal in life should be to achieve your own happiness.
https://amzn.to/2XyrpPf $3.50 Kindle $7.95 softcover

Values and Purpose Workbook
This book is about you. It's about time. After centuries of being told that nothing is about you, it is time to set the record straight. You are a unique individual and your goal in life should be to achieve your happiness. https://amzn.to/2XwlkTv $3.99 Kindle $8.95 softcover

www.robertvillegas.com

Christianity – A New Perspective on Jesus

These three books are based upon a new perspective on the life and person of Jesus. Based upon a new theory of the story of Jesus as an invention of the Roman Imperial Cult, these books add significant new evidence for this theory.

Unkilling Jesus

Starting with Atwill's Caesar's Messiah theories, this book explores the following questions. How was the story of Jesus's life written? Who was Paul and what was his role in the creation of Christianity? What was his provenance and did he actually meet the resurrected Christ? Who wrote Revelation and what was the document's purpose? Why was Domitian assassinated? Who was Clement and what was the nature of his relationships with Peter and Josephus? Were the Pseudo-Clementine materials really "pseudo"? Why did Saulus attack Justus? How were the gospels written? http://amzn.to/2itMCoO $3.99 Kindle $15.95 softcover

Domitian: The Final Messiah

The central goal of this book is to define the specific themes and concepts that make up Domitian's contribution to Christianity – in a sense, we are defining the specific Domitian overlay to the Christian materials originally developed for Titus. http://amzn.to/2yWMSlx $2.99 Kindle $6.95 softcover

Paul's Agon and the Mystification of History

Paul and Jesus are joined in one important way; the way of a miracle. They met on the road to Damascus while Paul supposedly pursued Christians. Jesus, in a sense, told Paul to get with the program and stop persecuting his people. In this incident, the Bible tells us that Jesus is already dead, and resurrected. This book argues otherwise. http://amzn.to/2zSDsuP $5.99 Kindle $19.95 softcover

www.robertvillegas.com

www.ingramcontent.com/pod-product-compliance
Lightning Source LLC
Chambersburg PA
CBHW070420290526
45791CB00005B/1773